Jagged Alliance 2

Jagged Alliance 2
Darius Kazemi

Boss Fight Books
Los Angeles, CA
bossfightbooks.com

ISBN 13: 978-1-940535-04-3
First Printing: 2014
Second Printing: 2017

Series Editor: Gabe Durham
Book Design by Ken Baumann
Page Design by Adam Robinson

*To my parents, who encouraged my love
of writing and technology.*

CONTENTS

FOREWORD

I DISCOVERED *JAGGED ALLIANCE 2* a year late.

It was a checkout line impulse purchase at Electronics Boutique, found in a battered, unloved box lying with the rest of the commercial refuse of the bargain bin. I was there to buy something else, something I can't even remember today. I grabbed *Jagged Alliance 2* for $10, based on a half-remembered review in *Computer Gaming World* and a gripping description of room-to-room fighting in a third-world hospital.

It remains perhaps the best bargain bin purchase of my life. *Jagged Alliance 2* blotted out everything else for the next few months, and I became like a crazy man, telling my friends at school about this amazing game that nobody had ever heard of.

But like a lot of great works, *Jagged Alliance 2* hangs in there while so many other games fade away. Fans like me loaned copies to their friends and watched as they fell down the same rabbit hole. I'd get phone calls: "Rob Rob Rob! You would not *believe* what just happened in my game. Remember I told you about the Russian sniper rifle I got…?" And then I'd get a blow-by-blow reenactment of a desperate, heroic battle at a dictator's SAM site.

Each encounter with *Jagged Alliance 2* is like a snowflake. In one game, the battle for a mining town is a bitter, World War II style streetfight. In another, it's a nighttime commando mission in which enemy soldiers are quietly dispatched with throwing knives and machetes. In another, it's a dark comedy, with the squad's resident klutz dropping a grenade at his own feet, somehow surviving, then accidentally head-shotting the medic who is running to help him. It's an "I'm not even angry—I'm just surprised" kind of game.

Only a year or so after its release, *Jagged Alliance 2* felt like a quintessential "they don't make 'em like they used to" fetish object. Many of its contemporaries marked the industry's transition into 3D gaming: *Thief*, *Half-Life*, and *Grim Fandango* seemed to signal a new era, and *Jagged Alliance 2* was all-too-plainly a product of the past.

So yes, *Jagged Alliance 2* felt like an anachronism seconds after the shrink-wrap came off the box. But why was it so different from its peers, at once behind the times and yet years ahead of them? Why was it such a strange blend of influences, like Frederick Forsyth by way of Borat? And why hasn't there been anything like it since?

The turn-based tactical genre almost vanished within a few years of *Jagged Alliance 2*, and the few games that attempted to carry the torch came dismally close to extinguishing it altogether. Luckily, *Jagged Alliance 2* was far more than a variation on a genre's themes. It was a game of enormous possibilities, a mid-90s RPG, a wargame, an adventure, and it remains one of the best treatments of insurgency warfare in gaming.

But understanding a game's origins requires understanding a whole host of factors that are only tangentially related to what the creative team did, including the technical limitations they labored under, the business model that funded their work, the sales environment the game would be entering, and the personalities of the team's individual members. Game development is a messy, compromised process.

Fortunately, *Jagged Alliance 2* has the perfect guide in Darius Kazemi. This book reflects not just his comprehensive knowledge of the game itself, but also his understanding of the developers' craft. This is not a book your typical game critic could have written, and few practicing developers would have the time, inclination, or ability to tell *Jagged Alliance 2*'s story so clearly or comprehensively.

While Kazemi is a connoisseur of the game, he's not filtering its story through rose-tinted lenses. He does not treat *Jagged Alliance 2* as a singular moment of creative magic, but as a product whose greatest achievements were also contingent on a variety of unique factors.

It's fitting that this story is a complicated one: *Jagged Alliance 2* is not a game of elegant simplicity. It is a defiantly complicated game, one so gigantic that it seems like it should collapse under its own weight… and yet it doesn't.

They don't make them like *Jagged Alliance 2* anymore. They never did.

Rob Zacny
Summer, 2014

INTRODUCTION

In November 2012 I read *Killing is Harmless*, Brendan Keogh's book-length look at *Spec Ops: The Line*, a big-budget military shooter game released earlier that year. The game is what Keogh calls a "post-*BioShock*" shooter: It attempts to be a reflexive, self-referential game that calls into question the madness of the shooter genre itself.

I did not like *Spec Ops*, and I liked the book even less. I felt that the book took a middling, confused game and showed it in the best possible light. Each bug, cliché, and bit of clumsy design present in *Spec Ops*, regardless of whether it was intentionally included by the developers, was to be interpreted as commentary on American imperialism, the shooter genre, or video game culture as a whole. Keogh seemed to set aside or contort the facts of the game itself in favor of writing a book that was not about the game, but about a game he wished he had played.

Reading *Killing is Harmless* left me with a profound desire to write a book that was its opposite. I wanted to write a book that looked at the story and the systems of a game, which took into consideration the economic realities that spawned its creation, spoke directly to its developers and publishers about the labor and money they put into it, and even looked under the hood at the code powering the player's experience. I wanted to write a fact-based book, grounded in reality. Of course, I set aside this urge as a pipe dream.

Six months later Gabe Durham of Boss Fight Books contacted me, in part spurred by a review I'd written of *Killing is Harmless*, and asked if I had any ideas for a book about a video game. Did I ever.

Given the option to write about nearly any video game ever made, I chose Sir-tech Canada's *Jagged Alliance 2* (*JA2*), an obscure 1999 turn-based strategy game for Windows PC.

Jagged Alliance is a series of games released between 1995 and 2001 by Sir-tech Canada. Other games using the Jagged Alliance name have been released by other companies, but this book focuses on the Sir-tech years. The series is about modern mercenary conflict. In each game you are the commander of a motley crew of soldiers of fortune, usually paid by some besieged group of helpless people to fight back against an unjust military or paramilitary occupation.

I picked *JA2* because it was a core part of my experience as an upper-middle class suburban high school boy. When I was 15 years old, I bought the October 1998 issue of *PC Gamer*, drawn in by a cover promising a list of the "50 Best Games Ever." (This is the same compulsion that would lead someone today to click on a headline like "17 Hilariously Inappropriate Typos.") Living in the suburbs and being too young to drive meant that I was constantly bored out of my mind, so the first thing I did after reading the inevitably disappointing cover story was boot up the CD of game demos that came with the magazine. One of those demos was for *Jagged Alliance 2*.

I played that demo for nine months, until July 1999 when the full game was finally released in North America. I bought it immediately, and was hooked for life. Shortly thereafter, incensed that the game remained unknown to even my strategy gamer friends, I became a *JA2* evangelist.

Just a few months after its release, I found a dozen copies in the discount bin for $0.99 each. (The game did not sell terribly well in the United States.) I bought all twelve copies and gave a copy to anyone I knew who seemed like they might be remotely interested in it. To this day, I will bend over backwards to twist a conversation about *X-COM* into a conversation about *JA2* because there is no game I want to talk about more than *JA2*. I don't want *JA2* to remain obscure. I want it to change people's expectations for what a video game can be. I want all future video games to pale in comparison.

And finally, I wanted to write about *JA2* because I wanted to talk to the people who made it. In the eight years I spent working as a professional game developer, the best part of being in that industry was getting to sit down at dinner with developers and listen to their war stories about working on some game or another. Fortunately, during my time working in games, I got to know Brenda Romero, who got her start at Sir-tech and was a writer and designer on *JA2* (credited as Brenda Garneau). She put me in touch with the rest of the team and made it possible to conduct the interviews in this book.

Unless specified otherwise, quotations in this book come from interviews I conducted by phone or in person with *JA2* developers. I spoke to the project lead, the principal designers, several programmers and artists, and even one of the game's publishers.

In the process of speaking to the developers and examining the historical record left behind in the source code, newspapers, and game magazines, I discovered something that should have been obvious to me from the beginning: There is no way to talk about a game without bringing your own interpretation to the table. Even "hard facts" require interpretation. The memories of interview subjects falter. Historical records contradict one another. People disagree on why decisions were made.

Even what happened is often up for grabs. At one point in his book, Keogh talks about a ghostly image that appears in a mirror, which to him was clearly an intentional reference put there by the *Spec Ops* team. I called him out on over-interpreting things. The image looked to me like nothing more than a graphical glitch. But when I recently spoke to someone who worked on *Spec Ops: The Line*, they told me, "Brendan is right! That image was supposed to be a hanging body, but because it appeared during a moment when we were streaming in the rest of the level, we were limited to a really low-resolution texture."

Well then.

THE HISTORY OF SIR-TECH

FREDERICK SIROTEK JR. owned a souvenir spoon factory.

Sirotek was a Czech immigrant whose family left their home country when a Communist coup in 1948 left the Siroteks, a property-owning family, in a dire position. He moved to Canada and started a construction business that was so successful, he nearly retired in 1969, at the age of 40. But Sirotek was a businessman through and through, and so business he did. In addition to continuing with construction, he diversified his portfolio. In 1964 he started with another businessman Commemorative Products Ltd., a giftware company specializing in the kind of souvenir spoons a tourist might purchase at Niagara Falls.

"It was a business that never quite made the grade in the United States," [Frederick Sirotek] recounts. "We had a relatively high-priced, quality product which American tourists were perfectly willing to buy in Canada, but the same American wouldn't pay the price for it in the US."

The poor profit margin drove Sirotek to look for ways to reduce production costs. The spoons required resin sands to be manufactured, and in the 1970s Sirotek came across Janice Woodhead's resin sand business based out of Ogdensburg, NY, a short distance from the Canadian border. Recently widowed, Woodhead had taken over the business her husband owned, but she needed a partner to help run it. Seizing the opportunity to get cheaper resin for his souvenir spoons, Sirotek became a partner in this venture.

Resin-coated silica sand is used in many industrial applications. In the 1970s, manufacturers used it in precision casting applications. Sirotek needed to purchase silica sand in large amounts from sand pits across North America. But between the 1973 oil embargo and the deregulation of shipping rates, there were enormous fluctuations in the cost of freight. This meant that Woodhead and Sirotek needed to recalculate freight costs on a daily or weekly basis, which was labor-intensive.

Sirotek realized that a computer program could be written that would calculate freight costs automatically. They had no way of knowing that purchasing a computer for this mundane task would lead to the founding of one of the first major computer game publishers, which would be helmed by Frederick Sirotek's sons, Norman and Robert Sirotek.

Robert Sirotek, Sir-tech cofounder and son of Frederick Sirotek Jr.:

When the Apple II first came out in the late 1970s, my father was one of the first to buy such a machine. He needed a coder and it happened that his partner's son, Robert Woodhead, was a skilled and able coder. Woodhead coded programs for a business joint owned by his mother and Fred Sirotek. The main cost component of this business was freight, and Robert was enlisted to code Apple II programs to automate freight calculations for customers among other things.

The Apple was a very expensive machine and not many people had it. Woodhead wanted access to the machine, which the business owners permitted him to do only after 5 o'clock. During the day he would code for us. And while he was doing his own thing at night, he ended up producing all these video games.

Woodhead didn't have a whole lot of business experience, so he approached my father for recourse. Ultimately my younger brother [Norman Sirotek] and I stepped in to help him sell video games, to great success. I came in about six months after it started. My brother and Woodhead were really the early players behind it.

[Woodhead] wanted to take an early prototype of a role-playing video game he produced called *Wizardry*, and another called *Galactic Attack* [a space strategy game similar to Mike Mayfield's unlicensed 1971 *Star Trek* fan game], and go to a show in Trenton,

NJ on a bus! And my father said, "We're not going to let you take this expensive computer on a bus down to Trenton! That's crazy!" He wouldn't let him do it, but my brother said, "Hey, I'll drive him down to Trenton, it's near Atlantic City, I'll drop him off, hit the casinos, come back, pick him up, everything will be fine." So he went to Atlantic City, lost his money in about two hours, said, "This is for the birds," and came back [to Trenton] and hung around the computer show, and it was like a mob scene! We had ten layers of people ogling *Wizardry* that Woodhead created. Norm said, "Hey we're on to something—we gotta do something with this." So they cut a deal on the way back from Trenton, and that was the birth of the company.

I joined six months later and we went from there. Who knew, right?

The two sons, Robert and Norman Sirotek, founded Sir-tech[1] (briefly known as "Siro-tech") in 1980, basing it in Ogdensburg. Woodhead would eventually team up with designer Andrew Greenberg to turn his prototype role-playing game into *Wizardry: Proving Grounds of the*

---

1   Sir-tech is referred to variously as Sir-Tech, Sirtech, SirTech in all sort of different authoritative sources, including game boxes and splash screens. Throughout this book it will be referred to as Sir-tech, which is what Robert Sirotek, the company co-founder, says is the correct spelling.

Mad Overlord. Wizardry was an attempt to translate the experience of a *Dungeons & Dragons* style pencil-and-paper role-playing game to computers. It featured rich graphics (for the time) and a first-person perspective, and was the first computer RPG that allowed players to control a party of multiple characters with diverse skills. The Wizardry series, and in particular that first game, was an enormous influence on future role-playing games. The game was a financial success for Sir-tech, selling particularly well in Japan, where its influence on *Dragon Quest* and *Final Fantasy* cannot be understated.

Throughout its existence, Sir-tech was strictly a publisher of games: It financed the creation and marketing, and until 1994 it relied entirely on external contractors to create the games. Like many game publishers in the 1980s, Sir-tech received games in the mail from independent developers and would then evaluate the games and determine which ones they wanted to distribute.

One such independent developer was Ian Currie, a Canadian working full-time in the railroad industry. In the late 1980s, Currie made games as a lone developer in his spare time, mostly practice games that he made for his own amusement and education. Currie worked out of a two-bedroom apartment, and converted one of the bedrooms to an office for game development. At the end of each night, he'd copy his current project onto a diskette and bring it in to his railroad job in case he found a few moments at lunch to work on it. He was completely preoccupied with game development, constantly mulling over some technical or game design problem.

At one point Currie hit on an idea that seemed like it had commercial potential, an arcade action-puzzle game he called "Chaser." In this game, the player is chased by a monster around a grid of tiles that disappear as you walk on them. The disappearing tiles require the player to be careful as they traverse the level, lest they end up painting themselves into a corner. *Computer Gaming World* would eventually call it a "*Pac-Man* for the 90s."

Ian Currie, Programmer/Designer, "Chaser":

Back then computer gaming magazines often listed all the different publishers on the very last page. I used that list to write to all of them and ask for a non-disclosure agreement first and then I sent "Chaser" around to all the publishers who were interested. I got rejection letters pretty quickly from most of them.

But out of the blue I get this phone call from Sirtech software. It had been a year since I'd sent them "Chaser," and basically they said, "We want to talk to you, because we've had this game around for eons and everyone at the office has been playing it for the last six months. There must be something there."

Robert Sirotek, Publisher:

The game arrived in our office, our submissions people looked at it, it was reviewed by the committee for new products, and it was rejected! But as the months passed, our people in production, quality assurance, marketing and sales, all these people in the office were playing this game submission that was rejected. And I walked around saying, "What the heck is that?" and they'd say, "Rob, you gotta see this Rob, it's so great, we're having a great time with it!" And this went on for months! And ultimately I started messing with it, and I said, "There's something about this, I don't know what it is but it's got that unique charm." So we called Ian up and we cut a deal.

Ian Currie:

I got a contract to publish the game, which would ultimately be renamed to *Freakin' Funky Fuzzballs*—not my choice of name but I was too elated to put up much of a fuss. I had to rewrite it in a different [programming] language and support three different graphics modes. On top of that, I insisted on supporting various sound cards. I did all this in three months and I almost had a nervous breakdown because I also had a full-time job—I was doing the work on nights and weekends. I finished it on time and didn't know that it was almost normal for games to be completed late!

But it was pretty neat, and it got me the experience of getting published reviews, and then I kind of shied away for a little while because I was so stressed out.

Freakin' Funky Fuzzballs was released in 1990. According to Sirotek, it ended up shipping "somewhere around ten million units" via OEM deals where the software was packaged with various hardware devices. You would buy, for example, a joystick, and it came bundled with *Freakin' Funky Fuzzballs*.

After *Freakin' Funky Fuzzballs* shipped, Ian Currie was burnt out and took a break from making games. He continued his job at the railroad, but found the work monotonous. "[My day job] wasn't challenging to me," Currie says, "and I'm the type of person who always needs a project. If for some reason I'm not creatively fulfilled in my nine-to-five job, I will invent something in off-hours that keeps me intrigued and challenged."

And so once again in his spare time, Currie started playing with a concept for a game that was nothing like his hit puzzle game.

THE GENESIS OF
JAGGED ALLIANCE

THE JAGGED ALLIANCE series was inspired by Currie's obsession with two games: *Command H.Q.* (1990) and *Eye of the Beholder* (1991).

Dani Bunten's *Command H.Q.* is one of the earliest real-time strategy games, predating Westwood Studios' *Dune II* (1992) by two years. The game is based loosely on the territory control model of the WWII strategy board game *Axis & Allies* (1981), which Currie played extensively in his youth. Westwood Studios' *Eye of the Beholder* is a *Dungeons & Dragons* computer RPG where the player controls a party of characters (and can trace its own roots directly back to Sir-tech's *Wizardry*). The game features a first-person perspective, and combat and movement happen in real time. *Eye of the Beholder* was the first RPG to capture Currie's imagination.

Ian Currie, Madlab Software:

I was not your average gamer in the sense that I didn't play many board games; I would get bored playing anything that took too long between turns. I had never played [pencil-and-paper] *Dungeons & Dragons*.

I was a very visual person, and I liked the 2D graphic adventure games. I didn't get into any RPGs at the time because they were very heavily stat-based and the graphics weren't that good. I wasn't drawn to them, so I never gave them a chance. But while I was at a trade show for *Freakin' Funky Fuzzballs*, I saw *Eye of the Beholder* being demoed and I thought, "Wow, this is really cool." It had very cool graphics. It was a tile-based dungeon crawler, but while you were turning from one direction to another, they built in a couple transition frames. It was real-time, and I thought, "Wow, I have to try that."

That was my first experience with a party-based RPG, and it certainly was the catalyst for wanting to create a game where you could lead multiple characters.

Currie wanted to make a real-time game featuring a party of characters with a territory control component consisting of a map that needed to be conquered by players, sector by sector. He played around with these concepts, building a tech demo of a few people walking around a screen—not an easy feat in the early 90s—and decided to develop a full-scale project.

How Jagged Alliance plays

Jagged Alliance (*JA1*, 1994) has a straightforward story. On the remote island of Metavira, two groups of scientists vie for the rights to control rare trees whose sap can cure otherwise uncurable illnesses. The evil scientists and their private security force have taken over the island by force. The good scientists have hired you to return the island to their control.

"You" do not have an avatar in the game. *JA1* has two basic layers of operation: the strategy layer and the tactics layer. In the tactics layer, where all the action happens, *JA1* is played from a "god's-eye" view: The player looks down from the sky at a squad of little pixelated mercenaries from something like four stories up with just enough graphical fidelity to make out their shirt color and their hair color. You control up to eight mercenaries, chosen from a roster of dozens, each with premade personalities and skills. On your turn, you issue orders: *Beth, go behind that tree, crouch down, and take a quick shot at that enemy; Doc, walk over to Grunty and start healing him; Wink, take cover behind the building.*

You end your turn, and the enemy makes similar moves against you—attacking, healing, and taking cover. The objective is almost always to clear a given sector of its enemy presence.

At first blush, the game is strikingly similar to MicroProse's classic *X-COM: UFO Defense* (1994). In fact, each game was developed without knowledge of the other, but *X-COM* beat *JA1* to market by nine months and so has gone down in history as the originator of the turn-based tactical genre. Like *JA1*, *X-COM* has a strategy layer and a tactics layer. But while the tactics layer is often similar, *JA1* and *X-COM* significantly differ on the larger matters of strategy.

X-COM's strategy layer largely revolves around building your base of operations and researching new technology that your soldiers recover in tactical battles. Because *X-COM* is a game primarily about defense, the strategy is interrupt-based: The player prepares as best they can, waits for a UFO to show up, and then figures out how to respond based on their own preparedness. *JA1* is a game about offensive strikes. Your goal is to retake an island from an enemy force, so its strategy layer involves planning toward your specific goal: How is our ragtag force going to get from point A to point B on the island, and what is the best route for obtaining resources along the way? The player needs to strike quickly lest they lose momentum. *JA1* has an "open world" feeling to it, whereas *X-COM* presents itself as a series of tactical battles with some very tough decision-making in between the battles.

The other major difference between the games lies in their respective storytelling. *X-COM*'s storytelling happens in interstitial scenes between battles: You pick something to research from a menu of choices, and then after some time a text box gives you information about the game world. Its soldiers, while they have names and nationalities, have no personalities and are in fact randomly generated bundles of statistics. There is a near-infinite number of possible *X-COM* soldiers. While it is easy for a player to develop attachment to an *X-COM* soldier, the attachment is usually based around the thought that a particular soldier has earned experience and a specific skill set and it would be a shame if they died. In contrast with *X-COM*'s generated soldiers, *JA1*'s mercenaries were each designed by the Sir-tech team. Each mercenary comes with a funny nickname, a quirky bio, stats that reflect their personal histories, and, in a very unusual move for the time, full voice acting.

For a quick example, take a look at Wink E. Dickerson. Here is Wink's in-game bio, in full:

> As a part-time member of A.I.M., Wink Dickerson, a former major league pitcher, has used his natural talents to our clients' advantage for years. Though

still plagued by poor target sense, he is by all accounts a gamer waiting for the right opportunity.

His stats are mediocre, but he can throw a grenade further than any other mercenary. While the bio doesn't explicitly state this, it becomes rapidly clear to the player that Wink is reeling from being fired from the majors and is hoping against hope to get his baseball career back together. When hired onto the team, he says, "Of course my agent could call any minute. But if he doesn't, I'll be on the next flight down!" If the player fires him: "Don't worry. I get sent down all the time," cleverly using a bit of baseball jargon that refers to a demotion to a lower league.

Wink is a weird guy, with a weird use for your team (dedicated grenade-lobber). He's got a memorable story. Characters like Wink have personalities that the player can get attached to. This attachment is helped by the voice acting. While the game's acting might seem cheesy today, JA1 was in fact one of the first Canadian games to use unionized voice actors, working through ACTRA, the Alliance of Canadian Cinema, Television and Radio Artists.

Shaun Lyng, Co-Designer, JA1:

We got professional actors for next to nothing on *JA1*. They dropped the price down to what we could afford, and we did it under a radio contract.

The characters, with their portraits, skills, personalities, and voices, are the heart of the series, and more than anything else make *JA1* stand out from its contemporaries.

Development

JA1 development began in 1992 in Montreal with a three-person team under the banner of Currie's development studio, Madlab Software. Currie first recruited help from Shaun Lyng, an acquaintance he'd known since childhood. Lyng was writing a novel at the time, and he asked Currie if he needed any help with the story for his game. Lyng began by helping on the initial concept, pitch, and design documents. They placed a newspaper ad looking for a digital artist, which a Concordia University film animation student named Mohanned Mansour answered. Mansour had next to no experience with digital art and didn't even own a computer, but Currie liked his illustration work, and Mansour quickly fell into the role of lead artist.

> *Mohanned Mansour, Graphics/Artwork/Animation, JA1:*
>
> [When I applied to Madlab Software] I brought Ian my drawings and my paintings. I'd painted a few illustrations in a book and was using that to

apply for jobs. Ian had a really good eye. He's a programmer but he's also an artist. He plays music. So he saw the potential, let's just say, because I didn't have anything on the computer to speak of at all. He gave me a diskette and said, "Here's a program, install it on your brother's computer and let's see what you do."

At the time I was living in the basement of my parents' home. I didn't have a lot of expenses, and I still had a year to finish school. So I said, "I don't want to get paid. I want to be a partner in this." And because they didn't have a big budget at the time, Ian said, "Yeah, sure! Here's a crazy guy who doesn't want to get paid, we'll take him on." So that's how it got started. [...] Mostly it was me doing all the tiles and animations and effects. The art was pretty much a one-man job, though Ian had a strong vision for the art direction.

Shaun Lyng, Co-Designer:

The thing that allowed *JA1* to be what it was was the fact that characters were an important part of the design from the very beginning. It was Ian and I, and Mohanned the artist, so when opportunities came up [to write] lines, there was a chance for me to spot them. [Later in my career], writing for other companies, it was more just fill in the blank, and I wouldn't see a lot of it match [the in-game action].

I wasn't in on any of the design stuff. That's what made *JA1* special: At that time, two people could be the brains of it and control what's going on. We were three guys in a basement when we started. Even by the time we were ready to finish with *JA1*, even with the extra contractors [we brought on to finish it], there was just no way to keep up [with the better-funded studios] anymore. Couldn't be done. That was the end of that era of guys sitting in a basement, especially with CD-ROM—now we have to get all this media incorporated into the game. And that was when Sir-tech stepped in.

The CD-ROM format was gaining in popularity while *JA1* was in development. Currie and his team at Madlab Software realized that they didn't have the resources to put out cutting-edge games as a small independent team. At the same time, Sir-tech was reevaluating their business model. Throughout the 1980s and into the early 90s, Sir-tech relied on hobbyist programmers to send them games, and Sir-tech would offer publishing deals to the ones they liked best. But when *Myst* was released for CD-ROM in September 1993, its enormous commercial success changed the landscape for games: Your average computer user now had a reason to own a CD-ROM drive.

The CD-ROM held almost 500x the amount of data as the then-standard 3.5″ floppy disk. More data meant higher fidelity art, animation, and sound—and more of it. All this extra media had to be created, at an enormous cost in terms of labor, tools (like 3D renderers), and training. Professional game development studios were able to keep up with these demands, leaving bedroom coders in the dust. Sir-tech found that the submissions they got from their usual stable of independent contractors paled in comparison to the games put out by their competition.

As a direct response to these new realities of game development, Sir-tech founded Sir-tech Canada, a development studio in Ottawa. They chose Ottawa largely because it was a major city where they could attract development talent, and it was an hour's drive from Ogdensburg, NY, where their publishing arm continued to operate.

In November of 1993, Currie moved from Montreal to Ottawa to be a Studio Director at Sir-tech Canada. The new development studio was not involved in making *JA1*, which was still a Madlab Software project with Currie at the helm. Technically Currie was working two jobs: one running Madlab and finishing *JA1* for Sir-tech USA as an independent consultant, the other working with Linda Sirotek, the sister of Robert and Norman Sirotek, to build up a team at Sir-tech Canada to work on other titles. (A year later, Currie and Sirotek married, with Linda taking his last name. She is referred to as Linda Currie throughout the rest of this book.)

At this point, Currie took advantage of free office space at Sir-tech and used his own money to add a few new members to the Madlab team. One of those developers was designer/programmer Alex Meduna, a newcomer to the game industry who among many other tasks coded the game's exceptionally devious artificial intelligence (AI). With the exception of Currie, most of the *JA1* team was new to game development.

Alex Meduna, Programmer/Designer:

I was a gamer since I was a kid, and Sir-tech was my first job in the gaming industry. I studied programming but that was just a passion until I stumbled across a little ad in a local newspaper that Sir-tech was looking for programmers. I had played some Wizardry games, and was familiar with them, but I didn't realize Sir-tech had opened a Canadian branch! I was in shock that it was the same company.

From real-time to turn-based

While the Jagged Alliance series is known for its turn-based strategy, for much of its development *JA1* was a real-time game. Currie was inspired by *Command H.Q.*, and wanted to emulate its real-time action. The switch from real-time to turn-based came during development, while playing with early versions of the game. He realized that directly controlling a squad of individual units in a real-time setting meant that managing any individual unit was extremely difficult.

Ian Currie, Madlab Software:

In a real time scenario where you are ultimately controlling more than one unit (or character), you are going to have to rely on AI a lot. That works fine for games that have lots of units—where the units can be considered expendable. But when you only have up to eight characters, they are a lot more precious.

I began to feel that it wouldn't be fun if your party members were dying while being controlled by AI, yet if the AI is so efficient that characters never die, there's no challenge. So I ultimately realized I needed to make the game turn based and give the player total control. If the character dies, it's really their fault; I didn't want them blaming the game.

I remember calling Alex Meduna in to say, "Okay, I've made this big decision. I want to change over to turn-based." He was just horrified. And I said, "No, I see the path in my head for how to do this: what code needs to be changed, what interface we'll need for moving around, deploying an action point system, getting the footsteps for the pathing to see how far you could move and all that." So we just switched it over pretty quick. That's how *Jagged Alliance* came to be in its true form.

The decision to move from real-time to turn-based play was motivated not by a desire to create a particular kind of strategy game experience, but by Currie's desire to create characters who the player would care about.

In a real-time strategy game with multiple units under the player's control, the designer can't expect the player to have fine-grained control over the moment-to-moment actions of each unit. If the player controls everything, they end up in nightmarish scenarios requiring perfect split attention between multiple simultaneous encounters: Unit A is on the north side of a map and Unit B is on the south side of the map, but Unit A sits around doing nothing while the player tends to Unit B. The solution to this problem is to give units some amount of autonomy: You tell Unit A, "Go to this location and defend it," and while that unit carries out your orders, you can then pay attention to Unit B.

While this is a great solution to real-time control problems, it poses new problems for character development. Imagine a character whom you have grown emotionally attached to: They kick ass, have great voice acting, tell hilarious jokes, interact well with their teammates, and you've leveled them up to become a powerhouse. You order that character to patrol an area while you take care of something else. You come back after two minutes and that character is dead. You feel robbed of something that you had no control over, and you reload a previous saved game.

There are some solutions to this problem that retain the real-time nature. You could make important characters invincible, which is what Irrational Games recently did with Elizabeth, the sidekick character who accompanies you throughout *Bioshock: Infinite* (2013). But that lowers the stakes and removes the need for strategy, turning your game into an action game and the characters into set dressing. You could have only one important character, which is what Blizzard did with the hero system in *Warcraft III* (2002). But that means you can't have a party of interesting characters, which was another design goal of Currie's. You could add a pause button to the real-time game, as in Pyro Studios' *Commandos* (1998). The problem here is that while micromanagement of units is possible, all units still move simultaneously and it becomes difficult to track unexpected outcomes.

Switching to turn-based control, where the player must micromanage every movement of every character, solves the problem elegantly. Players never feel robbed of agency. Mistakes that are made can't be blamed on faulty AI, which allows the developer to place characters in real danger. The player can control a large number of characters, and the game can show the player every important action that occurs on the battlefield, because those actions happen in sequence rather than simultaneously.

MicroProse scores an interrupt

In the summer of 1994, not long after the team switched to turn-based play, MicroProse released *X-COM: UFO Defense*. *X-COM* was an immediate hit for MicroProse, selling over 600,000 units of its original DOS release alone, not counting ports to other platforms.

Robert Sirotek, Sir-tech USA:

I don't know how much time MicroProse took to make *X-COM*. They may have spent less time in development than we did; I know that JA took a long time to build. We may have started earlier and released later. We had no idea that *X-COM* was coming. [...] When it hit the streets, we were shocked; we couldn't believe how similar a product it was, and of course they had a few months' head start over us. Because of that, they really took the market lead on this type of product. It was a devastating blow in terms of what the sales potential for JA could have been. But at the end of the day, we outshone them. Their sequels never succeeded whereas ours did.

Ian Currie, Madlab Software:

When I checked out *X-COM*, I just hated the UI [user interface]. I felt that it was clunky. The characters in *X-COM* were just names and more or less identical in how they came across to me and I didn't really like it. [I thought] I could do so much better than this, and in many respects already was!

When Sirotek speaks of "outshining" *X-COM* it's important to note that he means that from purely the perspective of progressive craftsmanship across the franchise, since the sequels that MicroProse produced never lived up to the first game. As game developers, the Sir-tech team can remain confident that they did better work than the teams at MicroProse. On the other hand, *X-COM* remains on "Greatest Games of All Time" lists, while *Jagged Alliance* languishes in obscurity.

JA1 was released in June of 1995. Sales were strong enough that Sir-tech immediately approved a multiplayer semi-sequel called *Jagged Alliance: Deadly Games* (*JA:DG*). According to Currie, *JA:DG* came about simply because he wanted to try playing *JA1*, which was a single player game, in a multiplayer setting. *JA:DG* was primarily a multiplayer version of *JA1*, and came with a short single player campaign consisting of a series of linear maps.

Despite working as Studio Director at Sir-tech Canada, *JA1* was a contract job for Currie. *JA:DG* was the first game that he worked on as a full employee of Sir-tech.

While the developers are still cagey about quoting sales figures, the general consensus is that *JA1* met but did not exceed sales expectations, though it sold fairly well in both North American and European markets. To this day, key members of the team believe the game could have been a runaway hit if *X-COM* hadn't beat them to market by about nine months.

MAKING JAGGED
ALLIANCE 2

WHILE *JAGGED ALLIANCE* and its follow-up, *Deadly Games,* were not blockbuster hits, Sir-tech believed it had something special at the core of the series. In North America and Europe, the two games sold well enough that the company decided to greenlight a sequel.

Sir-tech Canada began development of *JA2* in the second half of 1996, and the game was released three years later: in Europe in April of 1999 and North America in July of 1999. For the first time, Sir-tech Canada was working on two major projects at once. While developing *JA2*, the team was also working on *Wizardry 8*, the finale of the series that had propelled them to international fame. Team sizes changed over the course of development, but Sir-tech Canada was never more than about 30 people in size. For the last year of *JA2* development, the team had to "borrow" developers from *Wizardry 8* in order to ship.

As with the previous Jagged Alliance titles, Ian Currie headed up development. Early in the process he was lead programmer in addition to designer and producer, but he quickly backed away from programming and hired a full-time replacement, Andrew T. Emmons. Also around this time, Mohanned Mansour, the lead artist on *Jagged Alliance* and one-third of the original three-man *JA1* team, left the company to work for Westwood Studios.

The core game

In *JA2* you play a shadowy tactician who has been hired by one Enrico Chivaldori, the ex-ruler of the small nation of Arulco. Your task is to hire a small mercenary force to depose Queen Deidranna, the country's despotic ruler, who also happens to be Enrico's ex-wife. From your mission briefing, you know the queen is probably in her palace in the capital city at the southern tip of the country, and that you have to get to her somehow from your drop zone in the northernmost part of the country.

Like its predecessors, *JA2* is a 2D game played from a top-down vantage point maybe 100 feet above the action. Its overall aesthetic is "cheesy 1980s action mercenary film." (Think of Rambo's less illustrious descendants.) JA series programmer Chris Camfield likes to point to the Christopher Walken-helmed action vehicle *McBain* (1991, 4.6/10 stars on IMDB) as an exemplar of the genre. The game's color palette is full of greens, browns, beiges and tans—the colors of camouflage, with an occasional streak of blood red.

It's a very funny game, but not funny in the way 90s video games often were with their Star Wars references and endless puns. *JA2*'s humor is the dark humor of *Die Hard* (1988). Its cultural touchstones are action movies rather than Lucas/Lovecraft/Roddenberry/Tolkien fare, and it frequently references pop culture but never elbows you, saying, "Hey, we've both seen that movie—pretty cool, eh?" When the game's writing is over-the-top, it's speaking in its own assured voice rather than frantically clutching at some kind of external inspiration. There are no characters that proclaim "Yippee-ki-yay, motherfucker," but its characters have one-line quips that are often just as good.

The game can overwhelm players coming to it for the first time. There are dozens of decisions to make with no guidance from the game itself. After a few scant cut scenes, you have to manage money with no initial source of income, decide what territory to invade first, uncover and commandeer mining operations, carry out tasks for townspeople, and juggle a massive inventory of items of often dubious or unclear utility, all while keeping a team of mercenaries alive in a hostile territory.

What's missing is an in-game tutorial: In order to play *JA2* for the first time, you *must* read the manual. How else are you supposed to know you need to hire more than one mercenary? How else will you know that there is a child hiding on the first map who you must talk to in order to progress in the game? How could you possibly survive the first battle without the critical descriptions of how the battle system works? How in the world are you supposed to realize there is a story-critical letter in the inventory of one of your mercenaries, or that you're supposed to give it to an NPC unbidden? How would you even figure out how to use the rather esoteric "give" command?

The 50-page manual begins with a step-by-step walkthrough of how to recruit your first mercenaries, get them through their first battle, accomplish their first story goal, and recruit their first NPC. You're then cast off into the cold, cruel world with the following text:

> Good luck! Between Queen Deidranna and the even more sinister forces that lurk in the countryside, you're going to need it.

The four layers

Broadly speaking, *JA2* is constructed from four layers of play: the laptop layer, the strategy layer, the tactics layer, and the adventure layer. The term "layer" is one that was used consistently within Sir-tech to help developers distinguish between different areas of the game, and mirrored the way the game itself was written, with different groups of developers specializing in different layers of the game.

The laptop layer is a virtual laptop where most of the buying and selling of personnel, weaponry, and equipment takes place. This functions as a kind of home base for the player. It includes an email application that keeps you abreast of story events and e-commerce transactions, a web browser complete with its own hilarious fake internet, some files with back story you'll probably never look at, and a finance tracker that tells you how your operations are performing. The email application in particular allowed the writing team to add story elements cheaply, since voiceover work was not required.

The strategy layer is a screen that is dominated by a map of Arulco and a list of all the mercenaries under your control. Arulco is broken up into approximately 200 sectors. Each sector is one tactical map, containing its own resources, terrain, buildings, characters, and secrets. You assign mercenaries to multiple squads, order those squads to move to specific sectors on the map, perform inventory management, and give mercenaries standing orders like "get some sleep," "practice your marksmanship," "recruit and train a local militia," and so on.

A crucial difference between *JA2* and its predecessors is the ability to create multiple squads that move independently from one another. This means you can have small teams of mercenaries in many different parts of the country. You might have an "A" team of crack soldiers and a "B" team of support characters that follow at a safe distance. Or they might send two squads to take the same city, one from the east and one from the west. This one feature adds massive strategic complexity to the series. The strategy layer is where you will attempt to answer the question, "How do I get from the north of the country to the south in one piece?"

The tactics layer takes over when your mercenaries enter a sector that is controlled by enemy forces and a battle begins. It's where you spend 90% of the game: This is where your squad of mercenaries takes corporeal form on a (pseudo-)isometric tiled map, transitioning from tiny dots on a board into little pixelated people. This layer will be familiar to players of turn-based games like *X-COM*, *Final Fantasy Tactics*, or even *Fire Emblem*. Here you issue orders to individual mercenaries: *You! Enter stealth mode and crawl over to a cover position behind that wall, then lob a grenade overhead. You! Reload your weapon, climb on that roof, lie in prone position, and keep an eye out for enemies.*

The adventure layer happens when mercenaries are in a sector that contains no hostiles. It's mostly the same as the tactics layer, with three key exceptions: You are not in danger, you can speak to civilians, and you move in real-time. As in any role-playing game, talking to civilians uncovers information both important and useless. Some civilians bestow you with side quests, some provide flavor to the setting, and some can be recruited to join your cause. The adventure layer is surprisingly robust. Between mercenary and NPC dialogue, *JA2* features about 30,000 lines of voice-acted dialogue, which puts it on par with large modern RPGs like *Mass Effect*.

The game has a special relationship to time. While you're looking at the laptop, the overall game simulation is paused. In the strategy layer, you control the speed of time as you might in *SimCity* or *The Sims*: paused, normal, fast, very fast. In the tactics layer, the game has real-time controls until the first enemy is spotted, at which point it switches over to turn-based controls. The role-playing game that comprises the adventure layer is controlled in real time.

Progression

You proceed through the game mostly by blazing a trail to new cities. After a city is cleared of enemy forces, you must investigate the city by talking to its residents, who offer side quests that can lead to rich rewards. You'll then begin training a local militia to defend the city from the queen's forces, which helps increase the city's loyalty to you. Most cities have an ore-mining operation, and the foreman can be persuaded to divert the mine's funds to your cause, depending on the charisma of the mercenary who attempts to persuade him and the city's loyalty to you. While there is no official timer on the game, the mines contain limited resources and eventually run out of ore, at which point the game is almost impossible to finish.

Propelled by the need to make payroll each week, you push on through the country of Arulco, investigating interesting features on the map and generally moving towards the capital city and the queen's palace.

While *JA2* has many typical role-playing elements, it does not support a strategy of "grinding," where players aimlessly traverse a map fighting the same battles over and over to earn experience points. While fighting in a battle will cause your mercs' stats to increase, the potential cost of doing battle can be extremely high. Typically it only makes sense to enter combat in a zone if the zone is strategically important.

JA2 has what Raph Koster has called a "use-based" experience system, which is still found in some modern RPGs, including *The Elder Scrolls V: Skyrim* (2011). As Koster puts it:

The basic definition of a use-based skill system is one where you have a chance of improvement every time you use the skill. So everyone has access to every skill from the beginning [...] and as you exercise the skill, your chance of success goes up.

[...] And sure enough, there's plenty of tales of how amusing it is that the use-based system there encourages strange behaviors that do not fit the expected behavior in the game: people jumping everywhere in order to improve the stats and skills related to dodging, that sort of thing.

These strange behaviors abound in *JA2*. Most notably, it's not uncommon to come across a pasture of cows in the countryside. An experienced player knows to stop everything that they're doing, drop all their weapons, and punch the cow to death. The cow doesn't fight back, but punching it counts as hand-to-hand combat, increasing core skills like strength. As an added bonus, if you have extra medkits lying around, you can heal the cow for a probable boost in medical skill.

When you finally reach the outskirts of the capital city, the game suddenly becomes even more difficult, which can catch you off guard if it's your first time playing. The capital city is the first place you encounter full-size military tanks, impervious to nearly anything but rare explosive grenades and extremely rare anti-tank rockets. Many players quit here in frustration, especially if they've been using their explosives frequently and find themselves in short supply of critical munitions. It's one of the game's biggest design missteps: If the player was warned ahead of time that they would at any point face armored tanks, they might be a little stingier with their rockets. This is also the first place in the game where coordinating two squads to attack a sector simultaneously becomes a necessity, a feature you wouldn't even know about unless you read the FAQ in the back of the manual.

Once you pierce the tank defenses, you're treated to a capital city in stark contrast to the rest of the country. Almost all of Arulco up to this point looks like a bombed-out warzone, though you can tell that even in the best of times it wasn't a particularly opulent nation. But in the capital you see marble floors, gold statues, Grecian columns, and Persian carpets. There is a coliseum dedicated to man-versus-animal bloodsport, where the vicious "bloodcats" that roam the Arulco wilderness have been brought to the queen's home city for her entertainment. It's a fully functional Versailles in the middle of a war zone, with Queen Deidranna at its heart.

Much like *Far Cry 2* (2008), the game ends when Deidranna dies. There's no particular scripted duel to the death. You might find her sitting in her palace, surrounded by swarms of guards, or she might flee into her underground escape tunnel with her trusted bodyguard. Regardless, when you find her, she curses your name and opens fire. But she's just a corrupt politician. This isn't like other video games. She doesn't have a robotic exoskeleton. She didn't drink a serum that gave her super strength. She is one person versus your squad of six professional killers. Her death is a death like any other in Arulco, only with a lot of fist-pumping when it's all over.

CHARACTER AND STORY

JAGGED ALLIANCE 2 features an unusually diverse roster of characters. There are 62 playable mercenaries: Ten of these (14%) are women and fourteen (23%) are non-white. The white men on the roster represent a wide range of nationalities. That may not seem very impressive, but for a video game released in 1999, it was a refreshing change of pace to see a bullpen of fully voiced characters with their own personalities hailing from a relatively wide variety of backgrounds.

According to Co-Designer Shaun Lyng, the diversity was a practical solution to a problem: If you have 62 playable characters, the player needs to be able to tell them apart.

If the game had 62 white male career mercenaries, the characters would be more or less generic slates that you would project characteristics onto, like the characters in *X-COM*. In contrast, Lyng and Currie wanted to create characters people would remember for a long time. They didn't have a lot of room to work with. Characterization in *JA2* is limited to brief three- to ten-second audio "barks" triggered by certain events (spotting an enemy, getting shot, killing someone, etc.) and a brief character biography on the mercenary selection screen.

Shaun Lyng, Co-Designer:

There's so many [playable characters], and there's only so many ways they can say, "I'm shot." It's very difficult writing. It's just such a short amount of time to say things in. To layer anything with character and subtext using dialogue is almost impossible because the real estate you're entitled to is so short. It's got to be snippets. So that can get a little tricky, and sometimes you have to really lean on blatant stereotypes to get stuff done. The same goes with the bio. You have a paragraph to describe somebody, and anything else sort of has to be uncovered as people use them.

The player recruits most of their mercenaries from AIM, the Association of International Mercenaries. Once the developers had decided on an international organization, they felt that there needed to be an international flavor to the characters. As a result, mercenaries hail from not only America and Canada, but also Jamaica, Hungary, South Africa, China, Cuba, Russia, France–the list goes on.

Like in any ensemble story, some characters in *JA2* are better than others, and it's easy to see where the writers used those blatant stereotypes. Some are hilarious: "La Malice," a rough-and-tumble Québécois knife enthusiast, is clearly a loving reference to a francophone separatist archetype that Lyng and Currie encountered while living in Montreal. Others, like Buzz, a female mercenary whose ex-boyfriend's cheating has caused her to hate all men, are one-dimensional at best and at worst downright cringeworthy.

Despite the inclusion of some bad characters, there are so many to pick from that you can ignore the ones you don't like. In most games, man-hating Buzz would be the only woman available to play, and as a result would act as a dubious stand-in for all women everywhere. In *JA2* you have nine other women to pick from, including a Danish Olympic sharpshooter, a Jamaican auto mechanic, and a nervous French newcomer.

As with *JA1*, Lyng directed the voice acting for *JA2*, once again going through the Canadian labor union ACTRA. While RPGs contemporary to *JA2* like *Fallout 2* (1998) and *Planescape: Torment* (1999) feature limited voice acting, usually only during key scenes, *JA2*'s dialogue is fully voiced by professional voice actors.

Mercenary relationships

Some of the best moments that you experience while playing *JA2* come from the relationships between mercenaries. In addition to a character biography and skills, many mercs have a list of colleagues who they are predisposed to like or to hate. Most of those relationships come with pre-recorded dialogue that gets triggered when certain events occur in the game. Let's look at my favorite relationship in the game, a fairly complex one between Vicki and Gasket.

When you're about to hire a character, the first inkling you get of their personality comes from their bio. Vicki's bio boasts of her marksmanship and repair skills, and that she "spends her spare time managing Vicki's Vintage Automobiles, her own restoration and antique car dealership." She's a consummate professional, working directly for AIM.

Gasket, on the other hand, is recruited from MERC—the More Economic Recruiting Center, an in-game organization that functions as a kind of comic relief where you can purchase oddball characters that aren't particularly skilled but have wacky personalities. Gasket's bio says he's an elementary school dropout who worked at his father's gas station, eventually becoming an auto mechanic.

You might think Vicki and Gasket would get along, as they're both mechanics with a love of cars. But Vicki is a black Jamaican, and Gasket is a white man "born and raised in the foothills of Kentucky." If you have Gasket on your team and you try to hire Vicki, she refuses to join, saying, "Sorry, man. I can't in good conscience be signin' with ya. Gasket is such a racist. I can't lay down my life for someone who'd just as soon like to kill me himself." The simple acknowledgement that racism exists was rare for a video game in 1999, and it serves as a powerful moment amplified by the fact that your past hiring decision is now preventing you from recruiting one of the best mercenaries in the game.

You're now faced with a decision: Do I fire Gasket just to get Vicki on my squad? The question is further complicated by the fact that it takes 24 in-game hours for new mercenaries to arrive in Arulco. If you fire Gasket and hire Vicki, you're going to be down one mercenary for a day, during which time it's possible you'll have to fight one or two crucial battles short-handed. In this way, a simple clash between characters can force the player to make a difficult strategic decision.

And yet the relationship gets more complicated from there. If you play with Gasket, you learn that he's not just racist but also xenophobic (he hates Russians and Communists) and stupid ("As long as there's still a Russia over there in… somewhere, I say the Cold War ain't over yet!"). He also has a psychotic streak. If you fire him, he says, "I guess I'll just go back on home then and kill squirrels. Kinda too bad, 'cause people make a lot funnier noises." No wonder Vicki dislikes him.

But it's possible to get Gasket and Vicki on the same squad if you hire Vicki first and then add Gasket to the roster. And if you get them in the same room, it quickly becomes evident that Gasket has a crush on Vicki. He expresses his crush through the lens of his own intense sexism: "Vicki's such a babe, y'know? I mean… and she gives real good brake jobs." Meanwhile, Vicki has no tolerance for machismo. If you ask her how she's doing, she may say, "Why there be so many beer-swillin', testosterone-soaked slobs in this business? It's gettin' so a woman can't go into combat without bein' hassled!" Her only strong friendship is with Spider, another female merc.

If Vicki dies, Gasket howls, "Oh, man, Vicki, you're dead! You were the babe of all babes! I woulda killed ANYTHING for you! Now you're dead? Oh, Jesus, I swear I'm never fallin' in love with ANYthing ever again." If Gasket dies, Vicki doesn't even care enough to remark on the occasion.

Mercenary relationships in *JA2* do not have well-defined resolutions. The interactions exist to flavor the experience and to allow you to fill in the blanks with their own interpretations. These interactions only become apparent after hours of play, and only if you happen to choose Vicki and Gasket from a roster of 62 characters, and hire them in a certain order, and only if certain events occur. But the interactions are powerful.

Lyng and the other writers understood that if there is a complex underlying simulation, a writer can sketch the barest outline of a story and players will fill in the rest.

Mature content

Thematically, *JA2* takes a deliberately "mature" stance that was unusual for video games at the time. The game relishes violence, and violent deaths.

Ian Currie, Co-Designer:

For me, every time you kill an opponent, it's like a mini-victory and it should feel rewarding. I want the deaths to feel real and not mechanical. Seeing an opponent fall to his knees and topple over in death is cool, but not if it happens every time. So we devised unique deaths for very specific circumstances, like headshots and stuff that were very gratifying.

Like many "adult" games from the 1990s, *JA2* features heads popping like overripe grapes, leaving neck stumps spewing arterial blood out of some old Monty Python routine. *JA2* also contains sex, drugs, and alcohol. One mercenary, Larry Roachburn, whose bio states he's in rehab, is a Jekyll-and-Hyde type of character: If you make him drink alcohol, his personality changes for the worse, and his stats mutate so that he becomes essentially a completely different character with different skills. Certain versions of the game even let you hire prostitutes, resulting in a fade-to-black, a winking smiley face, and the sound of bedsprings.

Justin Hall, who reviewed *JA2* in October 1999, found the game's liberal use of swearing particularly notable:

> *Jagged Alliance 2* is one of the first games I've seen where the [characters] unabashedly swear. Not with asterisks; genuine cusswords. It took me many hours of gameplay, but one of my mercenaries finally referred to the [bad guys] as assholes. Meltdown, a mercenary known for her temper, called one of the other complaining mercs a pussy. After seeing many insanely tough gun-toting brutes tiptoe around naughty words, it is positively refreshing to hear someone who is supposed to be a killer swear when they [are] pissed off.

In addition to its elements of adolescent titillation, the world of *JA2* contains racism, sexism, xenophobia, government-sponsored torture, child labor, and extreme economic inequality. And yet it's difficult to say what the game's overall stance is on these issues. *JA2* is highly pluralistic, allowing you to play all sorts of characters from all sorts of backgrounds. That pluralism leads to a kind of moral relativism. While you can have a squad of friendly heroes who help each other as well as the downtrodden people of Arulco, you can also play as a squad of psychotic good ol' boys who ignore issues of social justice, seeking only to get a paycheck for putting a bullet in the queen's head.

JA2's pluralism is not an arbitrary decision: It mirrors the core Canadian value of multiculturalism, which evolved out of longstanding discussions of "biculturalism" that arose from historical tensions between Anglophone and Francophone Canadians. Declared an official state policy in 1971, multiculturalism is distinct from the American concept of a "melting pot" in that it is anti-assimilationist. Its central idea is that Canada welcomes people from all over the world, and encourages them to retain their own cultural, linguistic, and religious identities.

The Canadian multiculturalism of the development team was diametrically opposed to the distinctly American brand of globetrotting, gun-toting, justice-dispensing mercenary action that hardcore Jagged Alliance fans clamored for. As we're about to see, this contributed to compromises in both story and game design that make *JA2* unique.

MERCENARIES, GUN CULTURE, AND "REALISM"

SOLDIERS FOR HIRE have been part of human warfare since at least the Classical Greek era, but historical soldiers for hire are a far cry from the mercenaries we see in modern pop culture. Pop culture mercenaries are freewheeling, independent special-ops combatants. In the 1980s and 90s they were Vietnam vets; more recently they're Desert Storm vets. The pop culture mercenary brings to mind colorful characters like *Firefly*'s Jayne Cobb, *The A-Team*'s B. A. Baracus, or perhaps one of the action hero has-beens of *The Expendables*.

This is in stark contrast to real-life mercenary forces. Beginning in the mid-1990s, these groups have taken to calling themselves "private military companies" or "civilian contractors." They apply neoliberal economic theory to the military: In a 2007 Congressional hearing, Erik Prince, founder of the infamous Blackwater USA, said, "We are trying to do for the national security apparatus what FedEx did for the Postal Service."

Real mercenaries are terrifying private-sector military consultants, while fantasy mercenaries are modern-day swashbuckling scoundrels. We can trace this fantasy back to cowboy- and pirate-themed pulp adventures, and surely further back than that. But the direct progenitor of our image of the modern mercenary is *Soldier of Fortune* (*SOF*) magazine.

Established in 1975, *SOF* traded on fantasy as much as reality. It was filled with exotic accounts of armed conflict, jingoistic editorial content, conspiracy theories, firearms reviews, and, most infamously, advertisements for hired guns which led to many lawsuits and a handful of actual murders. Fred Reed was a writer for the magazine in its early 1980s heyday, and wrote about his experience in the March 1984 issue of *Playboy*:

> Popular myth notwithstanding, there aren't any mercenaries today in the accepted sense of the word: small bands of hired white men who take over backward countries and fight real, if small, wars for pay. The reason is that any nation, even a bush country consisting of only a patch of jungle and a colonel, has an army too big for mercs to handle. The pay is lousy, the world being full of bored former soldiers.
>
> True, there are shadowy categories of men who might be called mercenaries, but the word is hard to pin down. Are the hit men and cocaine pilots of South

America mercs? Are the Americans who joined the Rhodesian army and served with native Rhodesians? Men working under contract for the CIA?

So who reads *SOF*? Marines, Rangers, and unhappy men, mostly blue-collar, who are weary of the unimportance of their lives. What the magazine sells is a hard-core smell, a dismal significance, a view of life as a jungle where the brutal stand tall against the sunset and the weak perish. *SOF* may be the only one-hand magazine whose readers hold a surplus-store bayonet in the other hand.

And according to Reed, at the height of its popularity, "this den of caricatures [was] selling more than 170,000 magazines a month at three dollars a copy."

In a 1986 article, *People Magazine* referred to *SOF* as "a macho-adventure monthly," drawing a direct line to the "men's adventure" genre of pulp magazine. In the 1950s, publications like *Argosy*, *Man's Life*, and *For Men Only* would publish "true" stories, usually about men battling the forces of nature–or each other. These stories were like a mid-century version of reality television, and shared with reality TV its loose basis in reality. There is truth somewhere in the stories, but not without a lot of editing to make it palatable to a wide audience seeking entertainment. Founded four months after the fall of Saigon, *SOF* carried on the men's adventure tradition but updated it for the post-Vietnam War era.

In the 1980s and 1990s, as Americans learned to live with the psychic aftershock of the Vietnam War, Hollywood released a flood of films about mercenaries. As Robert Sirotek puts it, by the time the initial pitches were happening for *JA1* in 1991, mercenaries had "this certain sex appeal we were looking for. We were way ahead of the curve with that decision. Who knew that [the United States] would end up in so many wars?"

Shaun Lyng, Co-Designer:

[It was mercenary themed] from the first time we talked about it. I remember the genesis was Ian being able to get four guys walking around his computer simultaneously. I think mercenaries came up pretty quick and shooting came up pretty quick. Something involving a crew of people with guns. And it went from there.

Ian Currie, Co-Designer:

For some reason, and I don't know why, I sort of latched on to a more military type of situation. I didn't think of the fantasy thing where you can have magic and the various classes. I think that was my lack of experience, to be honest. I hadn't played that many RPGs. I'd only played *Eye of the Beholder* at this time. But I remember thinking, you'll have grenades for your spells, and you'll have ranged [attacks], and some melee stuff.

After *JA1* was released, the team realized very quickly that the game they had built appealed to a core audience of gun enthusiasts and self-styled survivalists. In the development of *JA2*, they tried to appeal to this audience by populating the world with a massive roster of "realistically" modeled guns. Programmer Chris Camfield was in charge of implementing the tactical layer battle mechanics. A lifelong player of pencil-and-paper role-playing games as well as strategy board games, Camfield instinctively turned to RPG sourcebooks (tomes of information compiled to assist role players in creating more vibrant worlds) for more detail, taking advantage of the meticulous research published by other designers.

Chris Camfield. Programmer (JA2):

There was a difference between the fan culture and the developer culture. When Shaun and Ian and Alex made *JA1*, they didn't know a lot about guns. That said, neither did I—just some things I'd read in books. I remember looking at the *JA1* code and the way that the gun damage was defined was your basic gun did 10 damage, the next gun did 12, then 14, 16, 18, 20 and so on. […] Ian and Shaun were really approaching it more from the point of view of trying to translate the experience of an 80s action movie into computer game format.

I used a couple of pen-and-paper RPG books about different guns to make it more realistic: Palladium Books' *The Compendium of Contemporary Weapons* [by Maryann Siembieda], and the other one was from R. Talsorian games, called *Compendium of Modern Firearms* [by Kevin Dockery]. Now that I think about it, there may have been numbers in there that listed rate of fire, cartridge type, and bullet grams. I think I tried initially to estimate the damage value of a gun based on the listed muzzle velocity of the gun and the weight of the bullet. [*Compendium of Modern Firearms*] also has all these different ranges of probabilities of hitting a target of a certain size or how wide the spread would be for bullets for a particular gun. That probably got factored into accuracy values. But those numbers still had to go through kind of a pass to make the progression better.

But there were still fans who were like, "Everything the developers did was crap with regard to weapons, the numbers should be like this and I'm going to go in and make it all right!"

Ian Currie, Co-Designer:

We'd get mail from people saying, "Oh man, I loved your game," and there'd be a photo of the guy's computer with a .45 caliber handgun leaning up against the keyboard. We realized that we had all these gun enthusiasts who loved our game, which was so ironic because none of us had ever even *touched* a gun!

The realism of games is precisely the realism of *Soldier of Fortune* magazine: Both *JA2* and *SOF* attempt to give their audience the feeling of what they *imagine* being a mercenary is like. Generally speaking, war-themed video games are perceived as being realistic, yet there are always three different factors at play: The reality of war, the fantasy of the video game, and the fantasy of war that is manufactured by the military, the entertainment industry, and the media. No matter what a war-themed video game claims to do, it inevitably simulates the cultural fantasy of war and never war itself.

The JA team was always trying to simulate "the experience of an 80s action movie," as Camfield says. One game system where this intent is laid bare is the game's crafting system. Oddly enough, the entire crafting system is an Easter egg that is available in the game but only obliquely hinted at by user interface clues. There's not a special menu for crafting. Rather, *JA2* teaches you that it's possible to combine, say, two half-full ammunition cartridges into a full cartridge by dragging one item onto another. You can use this mechanic (borrowed from point-and-click adventure games) to combine certain special items and create new equipment. Most items you run across in the game are strictly utilitarian like armor, weapons, ammunition, and medkits. But every now and then you find "junk" items, like an aluminum rod, duct tape, or a rusty old spring.

These items do nothing on their own, but if you're familiar with the 1985-1992 television series *MacGyver*, you might get some ideas about what you should do with them. The show's hero is famous for solving problems using little more than household junk. In a typical example, he "mixes pesticide, soap flakes and tile cleaner in a hot pan to create a smokescreen distraction." In a clear homage to *MacGyver* (whose protagonist works for a Blackwater-style private military think tank), *JA2* lets you combine a rumble pack for a video game controller, an x-ray tube, a pack of gum, a portable game console, and copper wire to create an x-ray device that can tell you the positions of enemies behind walls.

There was another, far more personal tie between the Jagged Alliance team and mercenary culture. *JA2* contains an in-game history of Jagged Alliance's fictional Association of International Mercenaries, which debuted in the first game:

> In a Montreal subterranean bunker in 1991, three men, known only by their aliases Colonel Mohanned, Commander Spice and The White Asian, found themselves in the heat of an armed struggle without enough access to manpower to

end the hostilities. With great effort, they secured financing and located the people they needed to put an end to the conflict.

This text references the origins of *JA1* in a Montreal basement in 1991, along with the core team of Mohanned Mansour, Ian Currie, and Shaun Lyng. In a couple of sentences, they managed to describe their origins as in-over-their-heads game developers working on a very large game, eventually gaining the financial backing of Sir-tech USA to help them expand their team and finish the project.

It's not hard to see the parallels between the fantasy of mercenary life and the reality of being a contractor in the video game industry. Contract game developers will often refer to themselves as "guns for hire." They are motivated primarily by money, working for whomever is paying—although many game developers take pride in their work regardless, much like the action hero mercenary with a heart of gold.

Balancing cultures

Despite core Jagged Alliance fans clamoring for "realism" in the lead-up to *JA2*, Ian Currie was already growing tired of its constraints.

Ian Currie, Co-Designer:

For *JA2* we said we'd [be more realistic], but at the same time I was already yearning for a little more escapism in the game. *JA1* wasn't a runaway success, nowhere close to *X-COM*, and I thought maybe it's because there's not enough escapism in the game. You come home from work and you want to play fantasy or sci-fi, right? Who wants to see anything realistic? I mean, playing mercenaries is an escape from your real life. But I got convinced that I needed more escapism, and that's what was behind the sci-fi mode.

Currie and his team added a series of quests to *JA2* that introduced the Crepitus, a race of giant insect monsters biologically engineered by Queen Deidranna that bear more than a passing resemblance to H. R. Giger's design for the alien in Ridley Scott's *Alien* (1979). These quests require a significantly different play style from the rest of the game. The Crepitus navigate by smell instead of by sight and sound, meaning that stealth becomes a matter of masking one's scent. The game's scent-based artificial intelligence is complex enough that a player can instruct one mercenary to stab another, and send the stabbed merc to leave a trail of blood to lure the Crepitus into a desired location. The high armor values and frontal attack style of the Crepitus give the player a reason to set their weapons to fully automatic and let loose a hail of gunfire—a stark contrast to the usual mechanics of sneaking, hunkering down, and firing pot shots at a mostly concealed enemy.

By adding these monsters to the game, the team hoped to provide a refreshing change of pace to the *JA2* experience. When the team released the demo of *JA2* almost a year before the full game's release, the Crepitus were included in a secret basement area. Fan response was not positive, and in the end Currie decided to convert the entire set of Crepitus-related quests, enemies, items, dialogue, and NPCs into a "Sci Fi" mode that can be toggled on or off at the start of the game.

In a parallel move, the team looked at the full weapon list Camfield had created for *JA2*, and decided that there were so many weapons that most players would be overwhelmed by the choices available. To combat this problem, they added a "Tons of Guns" mode, which like the Sci Fi mode could be toggled at the outset of a new game.

The team dealt with the tension between hardcore gun enthusiast culture and broader fan culture by allowing the player to enable or disable a large percentage of the content of *JA2*. This would never fly at most game studios, but it will soon become clear that Sir-tech was not like most game studios.

THE UNSEEN

In 2007, Gamasutra interviewed Harvey Smith about his role as Creative Director on Midway's *BlackSite: Area 51* (2007). Smith, an industry veteran who was Lead Designer on *Deus Ex* (2000) at Ion Storm Austin and went on to a Creative Director role on *Dishonored* (2012) at Arkane Studios, discussed how difficult it can be to create a game with a sense of place:

> With *Deus Ex*, we included fish in the water [...] rats in the alleys [...] cats on the rooftops. [...] I was recently adding a buzzard to *BlackSite*, and I wanted buzzards that wheel in the distance in the desert, and when you're driving along, I wanted, 20 yards down the road, buzzards around roadkill. As you get closer, they turn and flap and ascend into the air, and as you get closer, you realize it's a wrecked Humvee, and the roadkill is an American troop. That worked for me on many different levels. Some producer will look at that and be like, "Ambient Animal: Priority Four." And I'm just like, "You don't understand. This is really fucking

important. I can't explain to you why." And he's like, "Well, is it more important than fixing this bug in our animation system?" Technically, no!

It's critical to note here that Smith isn't lamenting a creative or technical difficulty. He's lamenting an *economic difficulty* in the creation of modern games with high production values. *Deus Ex* not only featured ambient wildlife but is revered to this day for the depth of its nonlinear, open world: there are secret areas, secret characters, and hundreds of lines of dialogue that you can miss the first time around.

JA2 was released a year earlier than *Deus Ex* and featured a staggering amount of content that players could not see on a single playthrough. The player chose from a roster of 62 fully-voiced mercenaries with their own personalities, skills, dialogue, and relationships to other mercenaries, yet in any given playthrough the player is likely to only ever use a dozen of them. The world has roughly 200 sectors that can be explored, yet only about 50 sectors are on anything resembling a "critical path" for completing the game. Players could make their way through the game dozens of times without discovering the secret crafting system, or without even trying the science fiction campaign. And yes, *JA2* contains its own ambient buzzards, which was novel enough to earn this remark from reviewer Justin Hall shortly after the game's release:

If you leave dead bodies laying around town long enough, carrion birds begin eating away at the corpses. After so many games where dead bodies just dissolve after being shot, this seems so smart. Duh—bodies don't just disappear. When you kill people, they lay there in a puddle until someone does something about it.

At some point between *JA2* in 1999 and *BlackSite* in 2007, this kind of development became economically infeasible. As graphics improved, art became more expensive to produce. Take a simple buzzard that feeds on a carcass and flies away when approached. A 2D buzzard in 1998 would have been a series of, say, 32x32 pixel drawings that may have taken an artist a day to draw, animate, and clean up. In 2007, a 3D buzzard would require concept illustration, modeling, texturing, and animation, perhaps taking two weeks of an artist's time. Whereas it was possible for Linda Currie to create 200 tactical levels (roughly one level every three days) for *JA2*, a level designer for a high-fidelity game in 2007 might spend two weeks to a month on the first pass of a particular level. In both *BlackSite* and *JA2*, a level provides 30-60 minutes of play, but because of its low fidelity, *JA2* can squeeze much more play time from much less development time.

Shaun Lyng, Co-Designer (JA2):

Well that's the price of being open-ended. If you take into consideration that some of these characters had massive amounts of dialogue and [most of the characters] might never be chosen [in one playthrough], that's where a lot of dead dialogue went. If you want to get the most out of it, that right there might get chopped today. Someone would say, well you can't have 60 awesome characters with written dialogue.

Alex Meduna, AI/Gameplay Programmer (JA2):

I'm not sure we ever questioned the effort we were putting into the hardcore AI simulation. In a lot of ways, we probably did go overboard in terms of spending too much time on details that rarely ever affected the play. Every so often something would surprise even us and it's because we'd gone that one extra step! [An enemy] will do something very intelligent and it's because they remembered they saw something three turns ago. The whole story of AI is that you can spend an awful lot of time and effort on this invisible thing that never gets really appreciated.

I think that attention to detail comes from the fact that we had a bunch of perfectionists as core designers. It made projects take four or five years instead of two or three years, and it was partially because we were so damned determined to pay attention to details, and to whatever we could come up with and justify spending the time on. It shows through not just in the AI, but in the interactions between mercs and people you'll [probably] never see. People who have played the game a dozen times have literally never seen half of the possible merc-to-merc interactions.

It's something you rarely see nowadays. Games are developed primarily as a business and to get back return on investment. The thing with Sir-tech is that was never our primary focus. We were never trying to get rich; we were always trying to make the best game we could under the circumstances. So we paid more attention to details that other devs would have cut.

Ian Currie, Co-Designer (JA2):

We had the luxury of making the game we wanted. Well, I was Producer and a Co-Designer! I answered to myself. I still had a boss in the form of my brothers-in-law, and of course they were very concerned about costs, release dates, all that sort of stuff. So there'd be some "come to Jesus" talks here and there, but for the most part I made the game I wanted to make!

And if Alex and I talked and agreed that something would be really cool, I'd say, "Yeah, let's do it!" We made what we wanted to make. Slightly naïve, maybe, but I don't regret any of it.

A lot of [the unique moments were] the direct result of me and Shaun being on the phone and laughing our heads off and me just making sure to implement it. I really believed there was a lot of value in surprises, the Easter eggs. I mean, I had my favorite lines that mercenaries would utter only in certain circumstances and things like that. And you realize most people aren't going to see or hear this, but the ones that do, hopefully it'll make an impression and they'll remember it.

Not only was Currie the Producer and a Co-Designer, he was also Development Director of Sir-tech Canada. At a modern big-budget AAA game studio it's unheard of for a single person to fill all three of these roles. Typically it's the job of the production department to keep the design department in check, as design is often concerned with trying to add more features while production is concerned with trying to make the game ship on time and on budget. But when the Producer and Designer are the same person, there is nobody in place to say no. Given this, it's not surprising that Meduna talks about Sir-tech as a place where "projects take four or five years instead of two or three years."

Of course, Currie still had bosses: his brothers-in-law, Norman and Robert Sirotek.

Robert Sirotek, Publisher (Jagged Alliance series):

Well, we were known for intellectually-based thinking games. We weren't into jump-and-run twitch-type stuff. We created products that had storylines behind them, that had scripts, that would be the digital form of a novel. An interactive novel. This was our forte and what we'd become known for, primarily through the success of *Wizardry*, which had all of those elements. When Ian was brought on as the head of Sir-tech Canada, it was clear that the type of product we would produce would be in that vein.

So Ian and I were on the same page from the get-go, so it was a natural fit to give Ian the lead in Sir-tech Canada. My brother and I knew what it took to produce great product. This is an art form. You can't expect people to paint by numbers and come up with an interesting picture. There is a creative flow, and there needs to be some tolerance to allow people the liberty to exercise their creative and artistic license.

We gave Ian that liberty. We were able to do that because one of the founding principles we had for Sir-tech USA was not to be beholden to anybody in terms of debt. We were self-financed—we were able to call the shots without worrying about pleasing investors. We were the only two guys that needed to be pleased. As long as we were profitable we were able to continue. [And] we were profitable in every single year; there was never any red.

Linda Currie, Co-Designer:

Part of Sir-tech's claim to fame as well as one of its challenges was that the games we made were massive RPGs. They were old school, and that's what we were known for, and that's what our audience wanted. Our magic ingredients were in these massive games, but they were also complicated to develop.

Developers like Meduna and Lyng were able to add tiny, surprising details to the AI and to the narrative because they answered to Ian Currie, who encouraged the practice. Currie was able to encourage the practice because he answered to the Sirotek brothers, who had unshakeable faith in his creative vision. And the Sirotek brothers were able to trust Currie because they answered to no one.

It's important to take a step back and realize how unusual this scenario is. It's easy to look at this story and think, "If more publishers were as enlightened as the Siroteks, we would have better games." But like Currie, the Siroteks were in a unique position that's practically nonexistent today in big-budget game development.

Modern publishers are large corporations whose executives ultimately answer to a board of directors. In the case of publicly traded publishers, they also answer to a legion of shareholders and the financial apparatus of speculative trading that values beating quarterly profit projections over making a profit (let alone making good products). At Sir-tech, the Siroteks were concerned with two things: staying in the black, and making good products.

The producer on Smith's *BlackSite* project who dismisses an artistic request as a "Priority Four" is not short-sighted and petty. The producer is responding to a system that has mandated a deadline for shipping the game. It's simply their job, and what the producer wants is reflected all the way up through the executives, the board, and in Midway's case, the shareholding public. If Smith wanted that art asset to get into the game and felt that it was worth delaying the release date for, he'd have to make a case that could be taken all the way up the chain.

Meanwhile, if Currie wanted something to go in the game, he could give himself permission and argue about it later with his brothers-in-law.

The end of an era

But Sir-tech's publishing strategy, which had worked so well in the 1980s, began to fail the company in the 1990s.

In a 1998 IGN interview, Robert Sirotek bemoans the lack of independence that crept up on so-called "mid-tier" publishers over the course of the 1990s. When asked a question about the increasing cost of marketing a game, Sirotek responds:

> [In 1992] is when you began to see real problems emerge.
>
> I personally misgauged mass merchants [such as Wal-Mart], the ramifications of them getting into the marketplace. A number of the well-known mass merchants out there embarked on a policy of requiring publishers to pay huge, huge money to be granted shelf space. And that's fine, we played ball on that basis.
>
> Because at first, in the early 90s, a number of them kept your products on the shelf for a good six months before they began complaining about a sales slowdown or whatever. And at least that six-month gap gave publishers a chance to coordinate their marketing initiatives, their advertising campaigns, their mailings—all of this stuff that can never be timed precisely.
>
> And we found last Christmas [1997] that many of these same mass merchants, who were willing to give you six months back in 1992, now would only give you three weeks to a month at best. You had to coordinate all these initiatives, create demand, and see your product sell in exceptional

quantities within that month before these people said, "Either mark it down or take it back." It's very difficult to operate in that environment.

Some of them in fact refused, even after we paid for the buy-ins—the tens of thousands of dollars we paid in August for shelf space for products due in October—these retailers cut their orders in half and didn't go as deep as we had anticipated.

That's what I mean by disrespectful. They have no concept of relationships. They just do what they think is best in their own short-term interest and that's the end of it. I don't think that's a healthy way to proceed for this industry.

So it's for these and other reasons, that unless you have the huge energy mass of an Electronic Arts, to be able to dictate policy to these people, it's really a losing game.

Sirotek is describing a power shift in the distribution of PC games. In the 1980s and very early 1990s, PC games were purchased through a variety of sources: mail order direct from developers or publishers, third-party mail order catalogs, computer trade shows, and brick-and-mortar retail. There were no national game retailers, so when people bought games "at the store" it could mean a mom-and-pop computer repair store, a regional chain, a tiny games section at a big department store, the adventure games section of a bookstore, and so on. With such a diverse selection of retailers, no single retailer held enough power to make demands of developers. Local chains had less sophisticated inventory management and profit models, so they lacked the laser-focus on moving product you see in today's mass merchants.

As the independent computer game merchants of the 80s disappeared or consolidated, so did the independent computer game developers and publishers. By the mid-1990s, stores like Electronics Boutique shifted their focus from PC games to consoles, and by 1999 when *JA2* was released, PC games that were not made by high profile studios like Interplay could be difficult to find.

As a result of these pressures, Sir-tech was unable to act as an effective publisher for its titles. In October 1998, Sir-tech USA (the publishing arm of the company, that originally contracted Currie and published his early independent work) announced it would be closing its doors.

Robert Sirotek, Publisher:

By the time *JA2* was ready for launch, the US company was beginning to have problems. Because we were an independent firm, because we were not a company with a huge profile the likes of a public company, we were having difficulties getting shelf space. Many stores around that time were trying to consolidate their inventories to a smaller number of publishers. It was decided the deck was stacked against us and therefore the best decision was to close the US corporation. That was a very painful moment.

Sir-tech Canada, where *JA2* was still being developed alongside *Wizardry 8*, remained open.

Of course, the landscape for PC game distribution has changed significantly since 1998. The release of Valve's Steam digital distribution platform in 2003, combined with affordable broadband internet, changed the way we buy games. Just as the fall of independent retailers went hand-in-hand with the fall of independent developers, the rise of digital distribution has come at the same time as the rise of the modern "indie" game. And while there are probably more differences than similarities between indie developers and the independent studios of the 1990s, when you look at most indie developers you see a structure similar to that of Sir-tech Canada in 1998. Indie teams are so small that the Lead Designer is often effectively also the Lead Producer and the Studio Director. The game industry has come full circle.

THE CODE

IN 2004, A company called Strategy First published *Jagged Alliance 2: Wildfire*, which was a standalone expansion of *JA2* featuring new characters and content that began its life as a *JA2* fan mod. *Wildfire* also included the source code for *JA2* and its expansions. This meant that modders were able to modify *JA2* to their heart's content, kicking off a dedicated *JA2* modding community that is still strong today.

Strategy First was kind enough to distribute the source code with a permissive license that allows the code to be redistributed for educational purposes, which means we get to delve into a couple of different fragments of the *JA2* source code. Don't worry—you don't have to be a computer programmer to understand what's going on here. This chapter attempts to illuminate the complexity of the rules that the *JA2* developers concocted for what seem like simple tasks.

Overview

THE SOURCE CODE for *Jagged Alliance 2* is written in C++ for the Microsoft Visual Studio 6.0 development environment (although given release timelines, it's likely development began in Microsoft Visual Studio 97). Developers were required to have two computers at all times, since they couldn't run the game and debug the code at the same time. *JA2* programmer Chris Camfield recalls, "You couldn't develop on a single machine [because the game was too resource-intensive] so you had to do it over the network. So you had a second machine with a second monitor, all so we could run the game in full screen and let us debug things. It contributed a lot to heat in the office in the summertime!"

The first thing you notice when you look at the *JA2* code is that it's divided up precisely into the "layers" that the developers keep mentioning in interviews. This is what the directory structure looks like:

- /Editor/
- /Laptop/
- /Res/
- /Strategic/
- /Tactical/
- /TacticalAI/
- /TileEngine/
- /Utils/

The **Laptop**, **Strategic**, and **Tactical** folders each contain code for their specific game layer. The **TacticalAI** folder contains the artificial intelligence code that determines how enemies fight. The **TileEngine** folder mostly contains rendering code that displays the buildings and terrain that you fight on. **Editor** has the map editor (originally a tool for the developers, later released to fans as well). **Utils** handles grunt work like displaying fonts, pop-up windows, and so on. **Res** contains a few external resources that are mostly inconsequential to the game itself (like the game's version number, and its icon).

Inherited code

Much of the code for *JA2*, particularly the tactical level AI, was reused and converted from the previous game in the series, *Deadly Games*. The conversion work was mostly done by Chris Camfield, who was fresh out of college when he started at Sir-tech Canada. Camfield was primarily in charge of programming and designing the tactics layer.

Chris Camfield, Programmer/Designer:

My first job there was relatively mundane. We localized *Deadly Games* for German and Spanish. I think I was switched back and forth between that and *JA2* in its initial stages but my memory of that is a little hazy. During university, I hadn't been playing a lot of video games, but what I had been playing then and before was a lot of pen-and-paper role-playing games, and strategy games of various sorts. So I really did have a good knowledge of different rulesets and how you might construct things.

I remember being confronted with vast amounts of Alex Meduna's code, like the AI from the first game, and struggling to understand it. It was fairly complicated. It was good code, but it was the first time for me as a developer coming to grips with an extensive body of code someone else had written.

Alex Meduna, Programmer/Designer:

On the first *Jagged Alliance* and *Deadly Games* I did a lot of tactical AI stuff. Chris Camfield took over my role for *JA2* since I had moved on to the *Wizardry 8* team. In the first year or two he'd often be over in my office, questioning me: "Why did you do this or that?" He took over my old code and modified it heavily.

Some of Camfield's notes from the *Deadly Games* conversion are still present in the code. Here are some comments from **TacticalAI/Attacks.c**, which is the file that specifies how enemy units decide who to attack next and how to attack them.

```
// CJC DG->JA2 conversion notes
//
// Still commented out:
//
// EstimateShotDamage - stuff related to
 legs?
// EstimateStabDamage - stuff related to
 armour
// EstimateThrowDamage - waiting for grenade,
 armour definitions
// CheckIfTossPossible - waiting for grenade
 definitions
```

These comments exist at the top of the file, which suggests that they are part of a larger organizing principle of the code. And we can see from the first line that "CJC" (Chris J. Camfield) is doing "*Deadly Games* to *JA2* conversion." These are leftover organizational notes that Camfield never erased from the code base. What we can assume from this, particularly the phrase "still commented out," is that the *Deadly Games* AI was mostly commented out to begin with. When code is "commented out," that means the programmer has marked it to be temporarily ignored by the computer, usually with the intention to "uncomment" it later on when the code is in working shape again.

We can infer from the list that at the beginning of development, the enemy units were not doing anything—they were just standing around—because all of their code was commented out. Camfield went through the tactical AI code getting small pieces of it to work in *JA2* until finally the whole thing was working again.

Let's drill down a little bit and look at that first note:

```
// EstimateShotDamage - stuff related to legs?
```

The first phrase, `EstimateShotDamage`, is the name of a function in the file. A function is a chunk of code that repeats a certain set of commands based on different input given to it. For example, you might have a `MultiplyByTwo` function: If you give it 4, it will give you 8; if you give it 10, it will give you 20. For the `EstimateShotDamage` function, you give it an enemy unit and a potential target, and it will give you an estimate of how much damage that enemy's shot will do to the target. In the game, the enemy will narrow their targets down to a few critical ones, then estimate damage on each critical target using this function, and fire their weapon at the critical target where they have the best damage estimate.

The second part of the note tells us that at some point, most of `EstimateShotDamage` was working, except for a possibly a leg-related part of the code. Camfield's note tells us that some portions of Alex Meduna's *Deadly Games* code were either not suitable for *JA2* or needed modification. Whenever a programmer considers reusing old code, she has to ask herself: Am I saving time by taking advantage of work already done, or is this going to require so much modification that it would be faster for me to write it from scratch? Camfield's answer was to reuse code, which tells us two things: First, that Alex Meduna's work was high quality, good enough to be used a second time instead of thrown out. And second, that Camfield's position as a relatively inexperienced programmer thrown headfirst into a complicated project led him to rely to on what was already there.

The tactical layer combat AI

Writing good artificial intelligence requires excruciating attention to detail. Even a mundane task like deciding which player-controlled merc to target in a given turn is the result of a long series of calculations. Imagine a flow chart that fills a wall-sized whiteboard and you'll get an idea of the complexity involved.

These calculations are so complicated that the developers can't keep them in their own heads. So the developers mark up the code with plain English comments so that any programmer looking at it could understand what's happening. Everything in the quotation block that follows is taken directly from the comments in the source code for the game's AI (**TacticalAI/Attacks.c**, lines 99-337). My commentary is in brackets, and I have cleaned up the spelling and capitalization a bit, and added some formatting for clarity.

Imagine a battlefield with your squad of six mercenaries against eight enemy soldiers (a small skirmish by *JA2* standards). Every time you press "End Turn," the enemy AI kicks in. Each of the eight enemies on the map will make the following calculations, and will loop through every character on the map, friend or foe, along the way.

Determine which attack against which target has the greatest attack value.

[Ignore a soldier if:]

- this merc is inactive, at base, on assignment, or dead
- this man is neutral / on the same side, he's not an opponent
- this opponent is not currently in sight (ignore known but unseen!)

Calculate minimum action points required to shoot at this opponent. If we don't have enough APs left to shoot even a snapshot at this guy, [ignore them].

Calculate chance to get through the opponent's cover (if any). If we can't possibly get through all the cover, [ignore them].

Calculate next attack's minimum shooting cost. (Excludes readying and turning.)

Calculate the maximum possible aiming time. Consider the various aiming times: If aiming for [a given] amount of time produces [the best] hit rate, [use that aiming time].

If we can't get any kind of hit rate at all [with our aim, ignore this opponent].

Calculate chance to REALLY hit: Shoot accurately AND get past cover. If we can't REALLY hit at all, [ignore this opponent].

Really limit knife throwing so it doesn't look wrong. Don't bother [with knives unless it's a really great choice].

Calculate this opponent's threat value. (Factor in my cover from him.) Estimate the damage this shot would do to this opponent. Calculate the combined "attack value" for this opponent: The highest possible value before division should be about 1.8 billion, normal value before division should be about 5 million.

If we can hurt the guy, OR probably not, but at least it's our best chance to actually hit him and maybe scare him, knock him down, etc., [then we have a viable target]. If there already was another viable target, how does our chance to hit him compare to the previous best one? If this chance to really hit is more than 50% worse, and the other guy is conscious at all, then stick with the older guy as the better target. If the chance to really hit is between 50% worse to 50% better, then the one with the higher ATTACK VALUE is the better target since he's more dangerous.

In our scenario with eight enemies and six player mercenaries, we have fourteen characters total on the map, meaning every turn the decision tree listed above is run 112 times.

The *JA2* tactical AI contains dozens of functions of this level of complexity. As AI programmer Alex Meduna notes, "Our game has a reputation for being a bit of a beast!"

The strategic layer AI

The *JA2* strategy layer consists of 41 files of source code, and the master file that controls them all is **Strategic AI.c**. This file contains 5,000 lines of code that create a kind of artificial dungeon master for you to compete against, in a sense simulating how the queen orders her army to respond to your movements inside the country. Once she notices you're a threat, she begins to upgrade her troops. If you take a major sector, she retaliates. The closer you get to her palace, the harder she hits you.

In addition to all the code, this file contains an unusual passage, reproduced here in its entirety: a 500-word essay outlining the general philosophical approach to the strategic AI. It's embedded in the code as a "comment"—yet comments are typically one or two lines long, and function only as written notes that go alongside code to help explain it to anyone who might have to decipher what it does. An essay-length comment is very rare, and usually reserved for design documents drawn up in a word processor rather than a code editor. To quote game designer Robert Yang's response to the news of this essay: "What a goldmine. All I see in *Half-Life 1* source code is 'hack' and 'sorry.'"

Here's a description of how the strategic layer AI works, written by an unidentified member of the team.

STRATEGIC AI—UNDERLYING PHILOSOPHY

The most fundamental part of the strategic AI which takes from reality and gives to gameplay is the manner the queen attempts to take her towns back. [Managing] finances and owning mines are the most important ways to win the game. As the player takes more mines over, the queen will focus more on quality and defense. In the beginning of the game, she will focus more on offense than mid-game or end-game.

REALITY

The queen owns the entire country, and the player starts the game with a small lump of cash, enough to hire some mercenaries for about a week. In that week, the queen may not notice what is going on, and the player would believably take over one of the towns before she could feasibly react. As soon as her military was aware of the situation, she would likely proceed to send 300-400 troops to annihilate the opposition, and the game would be over relatively quickly. If the player was a prodigy, and managed to hold the town against such a major assault, he would probably lose in the long run being forced into a defensive position and running out of money quickly while the queen could continue to pump out the troops. On the other hand, if the player somehow managed to take over most of the mines, he would be able to casually walk over the queen eventually just from the sheer income allowing him to purchase several of the best mercs. That would have the effect of making the game impossibly difficult in the beginning of the game, and a joke at the end (this is very much like *Master of Orion II* on the more difficult settings).

GAMEPLAY

Because we want the game to be fun, we need to make the game easy in the beginning and harder at the end. In order to accomplish this, I feel that pure income shouldn't be the factor for the queen, because she would likely crucify a would-be leader in his early days. So, in the beginning of the game, the forces would already be situated with the majority of forces being the administrators in the towns, and army troops and elites in the more important sectors. Restricting the queen's offensive abilities using a distance penalty would mean that the furthest sectors from the queen's palace would be much easier to defend because she would only be allowed to send x number of troops. As you get closer to the queen, she would be allowed to send larger forces to attack those towns in question. Also, to further increase the game's difficulty as the campaign progresses in the player's favor, we could also increase the quality of the queen's troops based purely on the peek progress percentage. This is calculated using a formula that determines how well the player is doing by combining loyalty of towns owned, income generated, etc. So, in the beginning of the game, the quality is at the worst, but once you capture your first mines/towns, it permanently increases the queen's quality rating, effectively bumping up the stakes. By the time you capture four or five mines, the queen is going to focus more (but not completely) on quality defense as she prepares for your final onslaught. This quality rating will augment the experience level, equipment rating, and/or attribute ratings of the queen's troops. I would maintain a table of these enhancements based on the current quality rating hooking into the difficulty all along.

In this essay, the author explicitly draws a line in the sand, placing reality on one side and game design on the other. It shows that the systems in place for the queen's strategies are not elegant simulations involving real-world resources like income and communication channels. Instead the queen's strategies are a smokescreen designed for maximum entertainment value. The queen's aggression is tied solely to the player's advancement. In fact, if the player doesn't progress, then the queen leaves the player alone.

It's easy to take advantage of this algorithm: After you drop your initial mercenary into enemy territory and kill the small security force that greets you, you can refuse to progress, instead ordering your mercenary to practice their skills. You can do this indefinitely, having your merc spend a year or more of in-game time in that first sector, training to become the ultimate mercenary.

While the algorithm is unrealistic, the game deploys narrative tricks to convince you that there's some kind of time pressure. If you dawdle, you get increasingly worried emails from the man who hired you, but the queen will leave you be.

The essay was likely written as an attempt to nail down the fundamentals of the queen's AI long before it was time to actually code it. The strategic layer was not really nailed down as a design until roughly the last year of the game's two-and-a-half-year development cycle.

Ian Currie, Co-Designer:

I remember one of the hardest things about *JA2* at the beginning of the design was coming up with what would be the strategy layer. I knew, and still believe to this day, that a successful formula is a combination of a strategy layer and a tactical layer, as well as the characters. [We kept asking,] "What do we do for a strategy layer, what do we do for a strategy layer," and mostly it was me talking with Shaun Lyng daily. Even though Shaun was not a game designer per se—he was a writer—he was one of my best friends and was a great sounding board. I think through talking with him on a daily basis we eventually came up with something that felt right.

Chris Camfield eventually came on and said "Let's bite off this, let's see if we can have multiple squads[2] and coordinate them and stuff, would that be a nuisance or would that be fun?" And I think it really

---

2   In *JA1* the player could only command a single squad.

worked out well, I think it's interesting to be able to get involved with that many more characters.

Some of my fondest memories of playing the game were like, "Oh my god, I really need to get my squad to here at this point in time." And it's down to the wire in terms of funding, and they get a random encounter along the way and now I gotta go in and fight this battle knowing I *have* to win or I'm in big trouble.

Alex Meduna, Programmer/Designer

At some point, they decided to transfer a lot of resources from *Wizardry 8* to *JA2* to finish it up, and it made sense to put me on it because I was so familiar with it. It was a relatively easy transition for me to make. I worked on it for somewhere around a year. By that time they made significant improvements in the engine, I was dropped into their strategic layer stuff, and it was underdeveloped and hadn't been fully thought-out and completed. Most of them had been focused on the tactical side of the engine, and the adventure stuff, so I took on the strategic stuff. The demo had tactical-level content because it had been complete for a longer period of time.

We ended up spending a lot of time on training the militia and the movement of the enemies on the opposite side. There's a very complex algorithm of the enemies moving around on the map. They actually spawn somewhere and move sector by sector. Because of the fog of war you're not privy to what's going on, but that was one of my big tasks, playing the role of the bad guy. How hard do you make it? It's always a huge debate on how challenging should it be. I always prided myself in trying to write very accurate AI taking into account as many factors as possible, whether tactical or strategic level. When you do that, you end up crushing all but the most hardcore players! So you do have to dumb it down.

One topic that came up often was sector recapture. When the bad guys take sectors back, the typical feedback is it's less fun to go back and win a sector a second time. We ended up having to make the same sacrifices as in coding some of the tactical AI while still making it realistic and making the enemy play effectively.

It's not that the average player is that dumb or incompetent. It's just that it's relatively easy to make a numbering-crunching computer be fairly ruthless and efficient, at least in a numerically analyzable tile-based, turn-based game where the AI has the luxury of being able to "think" quite thoroughly, versus a performance sensitive real-time simulation. So we could certainly make it gang up all the time on the weakest and most injured mercs, concentrate their fire, send every guy in the sector after them when alarm is raised, etc. But that's generally too deadly and thus not a lot of fun. So you have to put in a lot of artificial limitations, so enemies generally don't make the smartest decisions possible to them. There's typically a lot of randomness involved instead. As a result, they're sometimes surprisingly smart, other times shockingly dumb. The dumb can be by design, too.

The essay in the code is immediately followed by the definitions that determine whether the game is easy, normal, or hard. For example, the queen makes decisions every eight hours (simulated time) on easy, every six hours on normal, and every three hours on hard. On easy mode the queen will wait six days before sending troops to retake a sector; on hard she only waits two days. Instead of random encounters on the map ("there's a 20% chance the player will run into an enemy in this sector"), there are 29 possible enemy patrol groups scouring the map for the player. These groups have their own internal motivations. They can request reinforcements and equipment, they'll occupy a sector if they decide it's important, and they'll deviate from their patrol if they spot the player. When a patrol requests reinforcements, there is a built-in delay as they wait for the queen's approval or denial.

There is an incredible attention to fidelity to be found in the game's artificial intelligence. Yet the flip side of having enemies with their own individual motivations is that these enemies are often realistically bad decision-makers, which can sometimes make a game less fun to play:

Chris Camfield, Programmer/Designer:

Every AI character had information about the last position of the last sound they heard. They'd radio to each other, [causing enemies to swarm on the player's position] and it cost them action points to do so.

The downside of this was that there wasn't an overarching AI that would say "We should send three guys over that way." People would exploit the AI by going behind a building, firing gunshots, get the interrupt as the enemies approached, shoot the enemy dead, and then rinse and repeat until they'd killed as many enemies as they could get to leave their positions.

Without a master storytelling-style AI (the equivalent of a Dungeon Master in a game of *Dungeons & Dragons*), the ebb and flow of combat became a naturally emergent property of the individual actors making independent decisions. Sometimes, as in the case Camfield mentions, this results in easy exploits. Other times it allows for strategies that feel clever, not cheap: Stand next to an explosive barrel and intentionally make a loud noise, then quickly run for cover. When enemies approach the barrel, shoot it and dispatch them with ease.

Data and code

Modern games are engineered to be "data-driven," as Casey O'Donnell explains in his 2014 book *Developer's Dilemma*:

> Engineers invest significant effort into externalizing the interests of artists and designers. They construct means by which designers can adjust the parameters of design mechanics, even though these may change dramatically over the course of game development as the team learns more about what makes the game particularly enjoyable or meaningful. Engineers often refer to this abstractly as "data driven" design, but it's not just about honoring the data. The way engineers work also privileges empowering designers, providing alternate methods for constructing the game system that does not always require the intervention of engineers (who might already be stretched thin by all the demands on their skills).

Data-driven design did not become standard industry practice until a few years after the release of *JA2*. The 2002

Game Developers Conference featured two talks on the subject, one by Rob Fermier and the other by Scott Bilas, followed by a torrent of articles and conference talks about the subject in the years to come. By 2005, when I joined the video game industry, if your game code wasn't significantly data-driven, you were considered behind the times. Among its many advantages, data-driven design allows a designer to, say, change the amount of damage a weapon does without having to recompile the game's code. Compilation can take minutes or even hours, so if a designer needs to tweak a number several times, and needs to compile the game each time, the time cost can be astronomical.

JA2 is not a data-driven game. The code and data both live in the same place: the code files. If a designer wanted to change the price of a gun, she would have to open up **Items.c** in Visual Studio, change the value from 350 to 450, and then press the "Compile" button. Compilation time on *JA2* was probably around 15 to 30 minutes. What this means is, if the designer wanted to change the price of a gun three or four times in a row, the changes would take hours to test. Usually the result of long compile times was that designers became reticent to tweak values, settling for "good enough" since they had better things to do than wait around for half a day just to come up with a good price for a gun.

Partly due to these compile times, the prices for items in the game can sometimes seem arbitrary.

Another cost of data and code living in the same place is that it meant that designers needed to be programmers as well. Of all the developers working on *JA2* in a design capacity, only two of them were not also programmers: Shaun Lyng, who wrote the dialogue and story scenarios; and Linda Currie, who designed the game's maps, of which there are more than 200. Lyng was able to work in a word processor most of the time. Currie had access to a tool that took advantage of the only real separation of data and code in the game: the map editor.

Linda Currie, Co-Designer:

On *JA2* I was one of the members of the design team, and again reprised my *JA1* role in doing all the levels. Which was interesting because I was also Producer and Lead Designer on *Wizardry 8*. So that was always a little fun to juggle, and I'm sure Ian had some amount of grey hair added to his head, "When are you going to get those levels done?"

For *JA1* we had an external editor that didn't work in the game itself. It was cumbersome. For *JA2* there was a proprietary editor. That certainly helped, although at the time we had development on the editor and creation of the maps happening simultaneously, which is a recipe for disaster in many cases. Every time there was a bug or a problem—well, some of them were quite devastating, where basically I can't save and I've been working on this map for 45 minutes or whatever, and I'd be screaming across the office, "Heeeelp!" [laughs]

And how the map world came together in *JA1*, I had this crazy project of taking screenshots, printing them out, and pasting them together. I had a wall size map of *JA1* so I could manually line everything up [to make sure maps flowed from one to the next]. In *JA2* the in-game editor made that a lot easier.

The ability to make tweaks to the map and see them in-game without having to recompile the code made it possible for Currie to fine-tune the maps in a way that would have been impossible on *JA1*. This is due entirely to *JA2*'s separation of data and code for the map and enemy placement information: Without it, Sir-tech would not have been able to ship a game with a world four times the size of its predecessor.

Coding "sexism"

There is an optional quest in *JA2* where you're asked to "talk some sense" into a rambunctious family of hillbillies. The mission is meant to be a humorous but challenging change of pace from standard missions. The humor is a mixed bag, relying heavily on tired tropes— the family surname is literally Hicks, they stockpile weapons and alcohol, and their cosmopolitan neighbors complain about cow molestation.

If a female mercenary speaks to the family patriarch, the player is offered the chance to trade her hand in marriage for access to the weapons cache. In typical Jagged Alliance style, if you choose to go this route, a lot of your mercenaries become understandably upset, with at least one mercenary having a unique response if you marry off his love interest. The way the game handles this is through a character's "Sexist Level":

```
typedef enum
{
 NOT_SEXIST = 0,
 SOMEWHAT_SEXIST,
 VERY_SEXIST,
 GENTLEMAN
} SexistLevels;
```

It turns out that men and women can have various levels of the "sexist" trait, and men can have the "gentleman" trait. Women with the sexist trait and men with the gentleman trait get upset when a woman is married off to the Hicks family. Yes, in the *JA2* source code, a helpful note explains that a feminist character "hates men," rehashing a popular belief in the tech industry that feminism is a kind of "reverse sexism." This one decision is the only place in the game where these traits come into play. There's vestigial code that suggests there were more uses planned for these traits. For example, an "AIM_PENALTY_GENTLEMAN" variable is declared but never used. Presumably this would have been a penalty levied on "gentleman" characters if they attempt to shoot at women. Several male characters in the game have the sexist trait, but that trait never comes into play for men at all—again, it seems likely that the team may have planned for friction between sexist men and women on a team but never got around to implementing it.

Whatever the eventual reasons were for cutting out other uses, the fact remains that deep in the *JA2* source code, some strange social dynamics exist where most women are sexist and it makes them angry about arranged marriages, some men are gentlemen and they're also not too keen on arranged marriage, and some men are sexist but never let it get in the way of their work.

There is similar vestigial code for racist characters as well as a "hated nationality" for individual characters (so that, for example, a Jamaican character might hate all British characters). None of this factors into the game, but racism and xenophobia lie dormant within the characters, perhaps waiting for a modder to bring them to life.

JA2: RELEASE AND BEYOND

JA2 WAS ORIGINALLY announced for an April 1998 release, but the game was delayed a full year. A delay like that, which extends the development time of a project by 30%, is one of the worst things that can happen to a project, causing costs to spiral out of control. There's no single reason for the delay. Alex Meduna speaks of the studio's perfectionist ethos as the kind of thing that contributed to *JA2* taking two years instead of three. Linda Currie chalks up the delay to everyday project management problems:

Linda Currie, Co-Designer:

In *JA2* there was an area of the game that was particularly unstable. The coder on it was not a bad programmer, just inexperienced. As a result that part of the game was a tenuous construction. You'd fix one thing and sixteen other things would break. Not to say that was the only reason we ran into time issues. But it's representative of the kinds of things we encountered: One little thing here, one thing there, and before you know it, this tiny feature adds up to three weeks delay.

In some cases we'd have people crunching on *JA2*, and they'd be there all the time, going in on weekends even. They were gung-ho and passionate, but the impact on them was still the same [as if we had forced them to work long hours]. It still burnt them out and their morale ended up tanking. Even though some of it was self-induced, we didn't stop them from doing it at the time. Our thought was, "Great, you want to do all this work? Awesome, we could use the help." In hindsight, we should have told people to go home. You need some balance in your life.

"Crunch" is a game industry term for work done above and beyond a 40-hour workweek. Crunch labor is often unpaid, and has always been an extremely common practice in the video game industry. Numbers on crunch are hard to find, but one industry survey conducted in 2013 showed 32 percent of developers working more than 60 hours a week.

Developers crunched on *JA2* through the summer of 1998. By September, the rank-and-file team members were frustrated with everything from the hours they worked to the inconvenient placement of the only general-use office phone. They wrote up a list of labor and management related concerns and took them to Ian Currie, demanding that he address the problems or else the developers would quit the project. Currie felt blindsided and hurt by the list, but also recognized that many of the concerns were valid. He conceded to their demands. Today he describes it as an important growth experience as a manager. The team was happy with Currie's response, and development continued.

When Sir-tech USA closed in October 1998, Sir-tech Canada was five months away from finishing *JA2*. They already had a deal signed with TopWare for distribution in Europe (a huge market for strategy games), but they had to scramble to find a new North American publisher. It was and still is common for game studios to use different publishers for different regions of the world, since publishers tend to focus on developing business relationships on their home continent. A company that can market and distribute games in North America does not necessarily have the connections to make similar deals in Europe.

Because they had agreed on a deadline with their European publisher, *JA2* was first released in Europe, in April 1999. *JA2* sold well in Europe:

Robert Sirotek, Sir-tech:

TopWare put a lot of marketing behind *JA2* in Europe, and it was incredibly successful. They sold triple, quadruple what we eventually sold in the US. I have to give much credit to Jurgen Goeldner and his company, Softgold. We started working with Softgold in the early 80s. They released all of Sir-tech's products, and they did a great job translating them into German and in other languages. They were the ones that put down the footing in Europe for who Sir-tech was and what our products were. They did a fantastic job marketing *JA1*, and they laid the groundwork for the successes that TopWare eventually had with *JA2*. Softgold definitely made it easier for Topware to succeed.

Ian Currie, Co-Designer:

TopWare's producer, Frank Heukemes, was such a big fan of *JA1* but never felt it was localized well. So they took it upon themselves to do a really good localization job. They did tons of promotion [getting at least 100,000 pre-orders], and it was the number one seller for six weeks in Germany. So that was definitely considered a success.

Eventually Sir-tech Canada secured a publishing deal with TalonSoft, the strategy games division of Take-Two Interactive. Robert Sirotek, who, after closing Sir-tech USA, moved to Sir-tech Canada, wasn't happy with the way Take-Two handled the game. According to Sirotek, Take-Two didn't spend much money on marketing.

Sirotek chalks it up to the fact that Take-Two was a latecomer to *JA2*. Take-Two hadn't sunk a lot of money into the project, so they didn't see it as an integral part of their strategy as a publisher. The game released in North America in July of 1999 and according to Sirotek "met numbers" but did not exceed sales expectations. In the video game business that usually means a game broke even, recouping its costs to the publisher, but did not make much money for the developer.

Critical reception was strong. *Computer Strategy Games Plus* gave it 5 out of 5 stars, calling it "simply superb. It's detailed, it's engrossing, it's replayable, it's funny, and it's varied." It received 4.5 out of 5 stars from *Computer Gaming World*, and similar scores from across the enthusiastic press. Currie was elated.

Ian Currie, Co-Designer:

I was on a cloud. I had done exactly what I wanted to do. I cared more about the critical reception than I did any financial stuff.

I worked on *JA2* for the gratification of making cool stuff. All those Easter eggs? They don't do anything for the sales of the game. But they do create memories. I wanted something where people would go, "Wow, this is a cool game." I wanted them to get attached to characters. I wanted them to care if a specific character died and have to decide whether to reload that save game or choose to go on. I know that agony: "I can barely make it through this battle, I can't go back and save whats-his-face, I just have to accept his death." I was very happy with it in that respect.

Unfortunately, one crucial publication reviewed *JA2* unfavorably. *PC Gamer*, arguably the most influential computer gaming magazine of its time, gave it a score of 74%—much lower than most other publications. From the review's content, it was clear that the reviewer only played the first few battles in the game. News of the review hit the Sir-tech developers hard, and for many of the developers it's a negative memory that stands out to this day.

Despite its lackluster sales, *JA2*'s mostly stellar critical reception and one-of-a-kind game design earned it a die-hard fan base and a long afterlife.

The *JA2* modding community formed almost immediately upon the release of the game's single-map demo in October 1998. Modders hacked into the demo, inspected data files, and wrote editor utilities that would let fans tweak statistics and include weapons that weren't meant to be revealed until the final game was released.

After *JA2*'s release, the modding community flourished, especially after Strategy First, who purchased the rights to the Jagged Alliance franchise after Sir-tech's closure, released the source code in 2002. The Bear's Pit, a long-running forum for fans of the series, lists 49 player-made mods, many of which are "total conversion" mods that remix *JA2* into completely new games.

As for the official franchise, it's had a bumpy ride since *JA2* was released. A short standalone game called *Jagged Alliance 2: Unfinished Business* was released by Sir-tech Canada in 2000. Using the same technology as *JA2*, *Unfinished Business* is a series of linear missions with some new mercenaries, items, features, and bug fixes. It was warmly welcomed by the fan community but was nothing like the sprawling masterpiece of *JA2* itself. Notably, it shipped with a polished version of Sir-tech's internal map editor, which was a boon to the modding community.

After *Unfinished Business*, Sir-tech Canada closed and Ian Currie cut a deal to find jobs for much of the team at Strategy First in nearby Montreal. While at Strategy First, a small team of ex-Sir-tech developers worked on designs for *Jagged Alliance 3*. According to Chris Camfield, their design involved a far more complex strategic layer than *JA2*'s:

Chris Camfield, Programmer/Designer:

Instead of rebels and a dictator, there was going to be a multi-faction conflict. There was also a small island off the mainland, and whoever ruled that island was sort of a mad scientist who gave you side missions. If you completed enough of those he would launch an army of cyborgs and invade the main island. That was going to be our science fiction content. [laughs] We were going to get away from the player having to take over every sector. We were going to have a shifting border between friendly and enemy territory, where the player's actions would be a tipping point. Sectors weren't necessarily square, which would allow us to place locations for battles at key geographic areas. Maybe you'd go blow up a dam or take a bridge or whatever which would cause your troops in the local area to succeed. I think we had a lot of really good ideas in the end for JA3 but it just didn't happen.

Some development work was done on *Jagged Alliance 3*, but before the team got very far, Strategy First closed its Montreal development offices to focus exclusively on publishing.

In 2007, Strategy First published a standalone title called *Jagged Alliance 2: Wildfire*. Originally a fan-made mod of *JA2*, *Wildfire* features new characters, a new plot involving the takedown of a drug cartel, and scenarios that were far more difficult than those encountered in *JA2*. It received mixed reviews, with many reviewers docking it points for its frustrating difficulty level.

That same year, a small production house acquired the rights to make a Jagged Alliance movie, which never materialized. Meanwhile, a Russian game development studio released *Hired Guns: The Jagged Edge*, which was intended to be a Jagged Alliance game but had to be reskinned at the last minute when the studio lost the rights to the intellectual property. *JA1* was re-released for the Nintendo DS in 2009, but the fifteen-year-old user interface hadn't been updated for the DS hardware, and the game received very poor reviews.

In 2012, two completely different Jagged Alliance games were released by two separate development studios. *Jagged Alliance Online*, by Cliffhanger Studios, is a browser-based game of tactical battles in the Jagged Alliance universe that removes the strategy layer from the Jagged Alliance experience, focusing instead on tactical battles. *Jagged Alliance: Back in Action* is billed as a 3D remake of *JA2* that removes the strategy and adventure layers from the original game, and also simplifies the tactics layer. Neither game was critically or commercially successful. While they're passable games in their own right, they don't play like Jagged Alliance games.

A Kickstarter-funded game called *Jagged Alliance: Flashback* received $368,000 in funding from fans in May 2013. The game is developed by Full Control, a Danish studio with a lot of experience making turn-based tactics games. The studio's past games have received mixed reviews, but a cursory look at The Bear's Pit forums shows that *Flashback* is the next great hope for Jagged Alliance fans who have been waiting 15 years for a game to recapture the magic of *JA2*.

All these commercial ventures aside, there's a mod of *JA2* created by fans that may go down in history as the canonical version of the game. *Jagged Alliance 2 v1.13* takes its name from the incremental numbering system that Sir-tech used when they released patches for *JA2*. Their final commercial release was v1.12, and by calling this version v1.13, the modding community signals that this version is their vision of *JA2* as it was meant to be released, had Sir-tech the luxury of as much time and money as they needed.

As a kind of mega-mod, v1.13 has been in development since 2005 and is still actively developed today. The mod introduces hundreds of new features to the game. Some changes are purely technical, such as supporting higher video resolutions. Some changes exhume unused content, including recorded lines of voice acting that were included on the CD but not used in the game itself.

Many of the changes focus on externalizing variables that are present in the original game's source code and allowing players to tweak those variables as they like. There are numerous changes to the artificial intelligence on both the strategic and the tactical layers. Interface improvements, hundreds of new items, and a functioning multiplayer mode make up a tiny fraction of all the changes in v1.13.

The v1.13 mod is so ubiquitous that today, players who come to *JA2* for the first time are as likely to play the mod as they are to play the original game, and this is a mixed blessing. Many of the mod's changes are undeniably welcome—I certainly don't want to play *JA2* at a tiny 640x480 resolution. The level of respect that the v1.13 modders have for Sir-tech is plainly evident in the things that they choose to include. They could have included new characters from, say, the *Wildfire* expansion, but instead chose to exclusively fold in the characters from *Unfinished Business*. The main reason is that *Wildfire* is not a Sir-tech game but the latter is, and the *Unfinished Business* characters are considered canonical while the *Wildfire* characters are not.

And yet, for all its interface improvements, v1.13 is even more overwhelming to new players than the original *JA2*. The options screen alone is enough to give an average player a panic attack. There are a dozen new ammunition types that offer incredibly minor tradeoffs (cold-loaded ammo is slightly quieter but does slightly less damage). The game's action point system is retooled to allow for minute (the modders would say subtle) differences between hundreds of new weapons.

The artificial intelligence has improved, but only in the narrow sense where improvement means "smarter" rather than "more fun."

In fact, the fan modders' sense of improvement highlights the big difference between the Sir-tech team and the fan community. Sir-tech was not particularly interested in putting hundreds of guns in the game; the developers did so because the fans demanded it. They weren't trying to make a realistic simulation of modern combat. They were trying to make a "realistic" simulation of an 80s action movie. The developers spent a lot of time riding the line between realism and entertainment, but when it came to critical design decisions, entertainment always won out.

When he wanted to include a science fiction mode, Ian Currie considered the wishes of hardcore fans of *Jagged* Alliance and then more or less ignored them, telling the fans instead that they could turn off the weird monsters if they liked. The developers at Sir-tech Canada were acutely aware of the desires of their fans, but in the end chose to pursue their own vision for a game that they wanted to play. Their unique publishing arrangement with Sir-tech USA, while it lasted, allowed them this freedom.

The v1.13 mod is the perfect game for the fan who sent Currie a picture of a .45 caliber pistol posed next to his copy of *JA1*. But it's the game that Sir-tech

Canada would have made had the team been less sure of their own authorial voice, going to fans for design feedback in the "transparent" mode of so many modern crowdfunded games. For most players who want to try *JA2* for the first time, I recommend ignoring v1.13 in favor of the original game.

It's the original *JA2*, after all, that drew the modding community in the first place, and the original that makes us diehard fans ask, year after year: Why aren't there more games like *Jagged Alliance 2*? And we don't mean "turn-based tactical role-playing games," but games of immense scope with strong authorial voices, that allow us to telescope in and out from high-level simulation to low-level minutiae. Games that can withstand a thousand playthroughs and still retain an element of mystery. Games that have the special "something" shared by both *JA2* and Currie's early "Chaser" prototype that kept the Sir-tech USA office enthralled for months after they rejected it.

Where a game like *Fire Emblem: Awakening* (2013) offers personal relationships that live alongside tactical battles, *JA2*'s personal relationships form a complex feedback system with its battles. Where *X-COM* has a strategy layer that influences the equipment and skills you bring to a battle, *JA2*'s strategy layer affects equipment, vector of attack, time of day, team morale, NPC reactions, and more. *JA2* isn't just impressive for the vast array of things it tries to simulate. It's impressive because these aspects are interconnected, creating a game that is much more than the sum of its parts.

Still, *JA2* is the product of the talented individuals who designed and built it. We see the drive of the Curries and Lyng, the game's vision holders. We see Ian Currie, a producer-designer hybrid at the top of the development hierarchy. We see the funding of the Sirotek brothers and the unique relationship that Sir-tech's publishing arm had with its in-house development studio. For a few years in the 1990s these parts came together, creating an environment where unusual freedoms existed—the freedom to put elements into the game on a whim, to assume intelligence on the part of the player, to take an extra year to deliver, and to ignore advice from hardcore fans in favor of the intuitions of a bunch of Canadians who'd never laid their hands on a gun.

NOTES

The History of Sir-tech

Frederick Sirotek recounts his souvenir spoon business in "Ogdensburg Firm Creates Popular Computer Fantasy" by Daniel J. McConville. Massena, N.Y. Observer, Nov 19, 1987. Originally published in the October 1987 issue of Business New York.

Making Jagged Alliance 2

Raph Koster's explication of use-based systems: "Use-based systems," July 18, 2006. http://bit.ly/1pFLabC

Character and Story

Justin Hall's review of *JA2*: "Jagged Alliance 2 Review." Firing Squad, October 31, 1999. http://bit.ly/UBw3Yj

Canada's policies on multiculturalism: "Canadian Multiculturalism: An Inclusive Citizenship," Citizenship and Immigration Canada (official government publication) http://bit.ly/1lExagp

Mercenaries, Gun Culture, and Realism

Fred Reed recounts his experiences writing for *Soldier of Fortune* in "Life with Bob" in the March 1984 issue of *Playboy*, available at his website Fred on Everything: http://bit.ly/1k7Ax51

The *People Magazine* article which refers to SOF as "a macho-adventure monthly" is Joshua Hammer and Kent Demaret's "Want Ads in Soldier of Fortune Magazine Led a Blundering Gang of Alleged Killers to Their Victims," first published on May 26, 1986 and available at http://bit.ly/1oLqKBw.

Television hero MacGyver's recipe for a smokescreen distraction sourced from "List of problems solved by MacGyver" on the MacGyver Wiki: http://bit.ly/1ttqIBr

The Unseen

Brandon Sheffield's interview with Harvey Smith was published on Gamasutra on October 5, 2007 as "The Subversion Game: An Interview with Harvey Smith" (http://ubm.io/1oLrczR).

Justin Hall's comments on carrion birds from that same review at Firing Squad in the "Character and Story" chapter.

Robert Sirotek's interview with IGN: "Sir-tech's Last Words" October 16, 1998 (http://bit.ly/XfuPUl).

The Code

I've made the source code for JA2 available for public browsing at https://github.com/dariusk/ja2.

JA2: Release and Beyond

The industry study showing 32 percent of developers working more than 60 hours a week is Patrick Miller and Brad Bulkley's "Game Developer Quality-of-Life Survey," published on Gamasutra on March 18, 2013 (http://ubm.io/1kmzEFS).

English-language interview with Frank Heukemes available at German site Jagged Alliance 2 Basis as "Interview mit Frank Heukemes" (http://bit.ly/1ldxHGJ).

Computer Strategy Games Plus's July 30, 1999 five-star review of *JA2* was written by Robert Mayer and is available at http://bit.ly/1Az0rUf.

The Bear's Pit forums are the place to find player-made mods of *JA2* (http://thepit.ja-galaxy-forum.com/).

ACKNOWLEDGEMENTS

First and foremost I want to thank the developers and publishers of the Jagged Alliance series that I was able to interview for this book: Ian Currie, Linda Currie, Shaun Lyng, Alex Meduna, Chris Camfield, Eric T. Cheng, Mohanned Mansour, and Rob Sirotek. Every minute of recorded interview I used in has a corresponding fifteen minutes that were left on the cutting room floor. All of it contributed to my understanding of the Jagged Alliance series.

Special thanks to Brenda Romero, who was a designer at Sir-tech and introduced me to much of the core *JA2* development team. This book wouldn't exist if she hadn't helped me make those connections.

Thank you to my editors, Chris Dahlen and Gabe Durham, who turned this book from a pile of embarrassing scrawls into something that I could be proud of. And thanks to my other readers: Ryan Kuo, Ryan Plummer, Michael P. Williams, Joseph Michael Owens, Owen Faraday, and Ben Abraham. I have to thank Gabe

Durham a second time, for both his editorial guidance and for bafflingly asking me to write a book about a video game on the merits of an essay I wrote called "Fuck Videogames."

And thanks to my spouse Courtney Stanton, who provided crucial editorial, logistical, and emotional support throughout the year-long process of researching and writing this book. She also taught me that if I make a writing schedule and stick to it, writing will happen.

SPECIAL THANKS

For making this series possible, Boss Fight Books would like to thank Ken Durham, Jakub Koziol, Cathy Durham, Maxwell Neely-Cohen, Adrian Purser, Kevin John Harty, Gustav Wedholm, Theodore Fox, Anders Ekermo, Jim Fasoline, Mohammed Taher, Joe Murray, Ethan Storeng, Bill Barksdale, Max Symmes, Philip J. Reed, Robert Bowling, Jason Morales, Keith Charles, and Asher Henderson.

ALSO FROM
BOSS FIGHT BOOKS